CORONA-FASCISM

HOW POLITICIANS USED A VIRUS TO ELIMINATE PRIVACY, ENRICH THEMSELVES, AND PUT THE FINAL NAILS IN LIBERTY'S COFFIN

ALU AXELMAN

DEFIANCE PRESS
& PUBLISHING

CORONA-FASCISM

ISBN-13: 978-1-948035-07-1 (Paperback)
ISBN-13: 978-1-7372522-0-7 (eBook)

Edited by Janet Musick
Cover designed by Spomenka Bojanic
Interior designed by Debbi Stocco

Published by Defiance Press and Publishing, LLC

Bulk orders of this book may be obtained by contacting Defiance Press and Publishing, LLC. www.defiancepress.com.

Public Relations Dept. – Defiance Press & Publishing, LLC
281-581-9300
pr@defiancepress.com

Defiance Press & Publishing, LLC
281-581-9300
info@defiancepress.com

TABLE OF CONTENTS

AUTHOR'S NOTE

YOU WILL NOTE THAT I have used lowercase letters for the "united states," "u.s.," "one country," and several other terms throughout this book. Here's why:

After years of being a pro-America patriot who believed we could and should all unite under one set of values, I have come to believe that each of the 50 states is unique. No two states have the same cultures. New Hampshire, California, Texas, New Jersey, Wyoming, and Georgia are all quite different from one another, aren't they?

Capitalizing "United States" or by referring to it as "U.S.," "America," or as "one country" reinforces the idea that we are all citizens of one nation, meaning we all have the same value system. That is not the case.

INTRODUCTION

PLEASE BEAR IN MIND WHILE reading this book that it was written and submitted at the beginning of April 2021, a year and a half into the "worst pandemic in the history of the universe." Political news evolves in a matter of minutes or hours, which renders any political book largely outdated by the time it's published.

While I doubt corona-fascism is going anywhere, this book will almost certainly be somewhat outdated by the time it reaches readers. However, I believe this book will remain relevant regardless of whether corona-fascism remains intact. I am fairly certain that corona-fascism will never cease to exist; politicians may transition it into the next temporary or permanent crisis because their tyranny always requires some type of dramatic justification (racism, global warming, inequality, etc.).

Individuals in the united states have very little freedom. The amount of individual liberty has been diminishing and government powers have been growing steadily for decades. I want to remain totally open and honest. I do not believe, as some people do, that the world was perfect and that Americans were totally free until corona-fascism ruined everything. We were not free. The world had many issues, most of which were caused by politicians. The trend also demonstrated that politicians were increasingly violating our natural rights. The corona-fascism accelerated the trend and destroyed a lot of what made this world worth living in.

No, I am not a science-denier. I am not anti-medicine, nor am I anti-vaccine. I generally get the vaccines my doctor recommends unless I have a specific reason not to. After doing my research, I got the coronavirus vaccine. However, a part of me still wants to see much more data and years of studies and information to ensure that the vaccines for COVID are safe and effective in the long term.

I have tremendous respect for medical professionals, researchers, and all scientists. In fact, I am a scientist myself! At the same time, I recognize that many elites in medicine and pharma are in bed with politicians. This makes matters complicated because it causes us to doubt whether government mandates and contracts are influenced by these relationships.

Who am I? Am I qualified to write this book?

On one hand, I am just a regular old American cowboy with no college degree. To many people, I am unqualified to even open my mouth or have an opinion. Many people believe that I should be locked in prison or 're-educated' along with the other deplorables.

My name is Elliot Axelman, but you can call me "Alu." That's what my friends, my wife, my parents, and my three brothers and three sisters call me.

I began volunteering at my local ambulance service in 2011 right after graduating from high school with an Advanced Regents Diploma. I grew to love EMS, and I volunteered for around 30 hours a week at the station, which pretty much became my second home. The service sent me to EMT school in 2012. After getting my EMT card, I began to work full time as an EMT to pay the bills, and I continued to volunteer. At the time, I spent my free time teaching gymnastics and training in mixed martial arts.

I returned to St. John's University for paramedic school in 2013 and completed my training in 2014. The paramedic program entailed 12 months straight of intensive instruction of 16 hours each week. Concurrently, each student was required to schedule an average of 20 hours each week of clinical rotations throughout the year. The rotations totaled a little over 600 hours. Around 300 hours were on paramedic (ALS) ambulances in the NYC 911 system. The rest of the rotations were split between the many different units in the hospital. We spent time in the ER, Peds ER, ICU, SICU, Psych, OR, and other units.

My brother and I scored highest and second-highest on each assignment and finished as #1 and #2 in the class with the highest averages and final test scores. Of the 24 students in the program, two passed the final exam (my brother and I), though four others passed once the staff curved the grades and allowed for retests. By the end of the program, six out of 24 students had survived. That 25% passing rate is typical from what I've seen from other paramedic programs, as well. When I met my wife a year after graduating, she told me she was also part of the minority of the students who passed her paramedic program. That group was also exactly 25%.

What do paramedics do?

We work on ambulances, along with EMTs and advanced EMTs.

In addition to standard trauma care and transport to an ER or other facility, EMTs can administer oxygen, place some supraglottic airways, ventilate patients, administer aspirin, epinephrine, albuterol, and a few other treatments.

Paramedics can administer all of the standard emergency medications (25-60 medications, depending on the city) via the oral route, IV, IO, IM, IN, and sometimes via other routes, such as ET or SQ.

Paramedics can intubate patients and perform advanced invasive procedures such as cricothyrotomies, thoracotomies, and many others, depending on the local protocols. Paramedics interpret 4-lead and 12-lead EKGs. We use our cardiac monitors to manually pace a patient whose heart rate is too slow, cardiovert a patient whose heart rate is too fast, and we can defibrillate patients in cardiac arrest.

A good paramedic is worth his or her weight in gold. Similar to nurses and many others, each paramedic is unique. Some are incompetent, some are arrogant jerks, and some are superstars who can save countless lives in their sleep. Depending on the context and the individual provider, your best bet in a true emergency might be a good ER doctor, and it might be a great paramedic.

In 2017, my brother and I took an FP-C course and passed the test, which certified us to work as flight and critical-care paramedics. The few people in the united states with this certification can transport critical patients on multiple potent IV infusions, advanced equipment such as balloon pumps, some special ventilator settings, and can work on helicopters, airplanes, and critical care ground ambulances. Only a few thousand individuals in the united states are flight paramedic certified. My brother actually worked on airplanes for critical flight transport and on helicopters for critical flight transport and critical 911 rescue missions.

Before moving out west, my brother was a paramedic instructor at St. John's University. My brother and I are lifelong learners and teachers. We have both been field training officers in nearly all of our jobs, and we both did teach EMS at various institutes. We both also taught gymnastics, parkour, and martial arts tricking. At the time of this writing, I am also a NASM-certified personal trainer, specializing in martial arts, self-defense, power-lifting, flexibility, and sports exercise.

My résumé is not nearly as impressive as my brother's. He was intensely courted by St. John's University to teach at their paramedic program, which is considered the best one in the region, and whose instructors are all eminently qualified and experienced.

My résumé includes volunteering for a few years as an EMT, ultimately resigning as a lieutenant due to paramedic school taking up all of my time. I worked as an EMT for two years in a company that primarily handled inter-facility transports, though we did do some 911 response. I have worked as a paramedic since the middle of 2014 until today. During that time, I have worked in many transport and 911 systems, providing primary 911 coverage in the Bronx, Queens, Brooklyn, Manhattan, Yonkers, Mount Vernon, New Rochelle, Lynbrook, and many other towns. I worked in many transport systems, often transporting critical patients along with staff from the NYU Langone PICU, the Montefiore perfusionist (ECMO) teams, and many others. As strange as it sounds, working 911 in the Bronx was one of my more laid back jobs.

Oftentimes, we would be called to a nursing home for a sick and elderly person who should have been attended to much earlier. By the time nursing staff realizes that a patient is sick or struggling to breathe, it's often very late or too late. So we treated many patients who were extremely close to dying from respiratory failure (or any other cause). I have turned many patients around using BiPAP, intubation, or other treatments. My brother, my wife, and many friends have done these things even more than I have. While working 911 in Queens, my brother was intubating patients (mostly cardiac arrests) on a weekly basis.

Personally, I dislike the term "save lives" because I do not understand what it means. If a person is alive, it's really hard to know if you saved them from dying. They may have died if you hadn't intervened. They may have lived for weeks without you. They may have lived for a few hours. It's pretty much impossible to know for sure. I could say that some patients likely would have gone into cardiac arrest if I hadn't intervened and if they received no treatment for a few more hours. But I very rarely credit myself for "saving" a life. When a person is in cardiac arrest (clinically dead with no heartbeat) and I bring them back to life, that is not really "saving" a life, either. That is an example of bringing back a person from the dead. In fact, some systems refer to this as "resurrection." I have brought many patients back to life from cardiac arrest, and my brother and friends have done so hundreds or thousands of times.

In a cardiac arrest, paramedics generally do the same things for patients as ER physicians and nurses do. They ensure that proper CPR is being performed and that pads are on the patient. They attempt defibrillation, if appropriate, every few minutes. They administer the ACLS-recommended medications for the situation. They place advanced airways and ventilate the patient with oxygen, gain IV access, and consider any reversible causes of death. If a patient is not viable after a full resuscitation attempt, a paramedic can pronounce the time of the death and terminate CPR efforts, just like a doctor.

I have treated thousands of patients with difficulty breathing. Many of these patients' problems were pulmonary in nature, many were cardiac, and many arose from other pathologies (anaphylaxis, trauma, stroke, etc.).

I tell you all of this to give you a little bit of background regarding my medical experience. I am not a doctor. I am certainly not an immunologist, pathologist, or pulmonologist. I am also not a pharmacist.

I believe there is certainly a place for experts in public policy and in the discussion of medicine. I also believe that research, studies, data, facts, logic, and common sense are important. I believe that, as far as governments and laws are concerned, individual liberty is paramount.

For those who may be reading this in an era far in the future, I'd like to paint a picture of what the world currently looks like as I write this. Nearly every establishment in the united states requires a mask. Most seem to also enforce social distancing. Some even require eye protection. Many businesses have been closed temporarily or permanently by the restrictions that forced them to decrease their capacity or hours of operation. Most business owners resent the restrictions.

However, many business owners have been pressuring their governments for such restrictions. Why? Because employees could refuse to work and could legally receive unemployment if their employers refused to implement the CDC-recommended restrictions. So, employers were coerced by the government to beg for corona-fascism. This brings us to perhaps the most disturbing facet of the entire corona-fascism nightmare: governments of all levels have infiltrated and influenced business in so many ways that they are essentially one and the same. Hence the "fascism" part.

While I am a voluntaryist and a free market absolutist, I find myself increasingly supporting policies that would prohibit (formerly "private") businesses from forcing their customers to wear masks or get vaccines. I have long debated conservative and libertarian political analysts like Ed Mazlish, a brilliant attorney who is part of my team at The Liberty Block. At the time of this writing, he has totally won me over to his way of thinking. For years, we debated the premise of free-market absolutism and the uncomfortable reality that no business was truly private anymore.

All business owners in the united states comply with millions of laws because they fear being punished by men with guns (police) AND they observe cultural norms created by politicians and their cronies via a massive array of political and cultural pressures. For instance, if governmental mask mandates were eliminated today, a large percentage of private businesses would continue to require masks because politicians successfully convinced them that COVID is the biggest threat to humanity in world history. Ed and many others argue that capitalists should not sell the enemy the rope they know will be used to hang them. We have seen that private and government enterprises have merged into one disturbing beast with many heads, which violates human freedom and individual rights. We can't argue about free-market capitalism and property rights if we don't have a free market or property rights. Posited another way, the argument of free market absolutism cannot be made unless we have an absolutely free market. And the billions of governmental regulations on the economy demonstrate that our market is nearly the polar opposite of "free."

Over the years, Ed and others have worn me down and won me over to their side. I now believe that, because the government is so deeply involved in every business in the united states, I no longer have a major issue with opposing and restricting those businesses. Make no mistake; my greatest wish is still for the total elimination of coercion (the primary function of government) but, in the practical and real world, I think I'd live better with myself if I supported a restriction on a fascist (public-private) enterprise.

Getting back to what the world around me currently looks like: Hospitals remain as calm and empty as ever, but corona-fascism remains in force. Regularly, I am still accosted by nurses and doctors if I or my patient allow our masks to slip beneath our noses or if we are caught without one, heaven forbid. If I mention to the nosey nurse that my patient had COVID months ago, got the vaccine, and tested negative for COVID two minutes ago, I am still forced by the nurse to muzzle my patient, even if it compromises that patient's breathing.

Patients are still denied albuterol, ipratropium, BiPAP, and other treatments that could potentially expose "health care heroes" to the same air they exhaled.

Some hospital staff, on the other hand, have relaxed somewhat and allowed their masks to hang down around their chins for hours on end while at their workstations. Maybe they figure that, if COVID has been 'raging' for a year and a half and has barely caused any harm to patients as far as they could tell, they would survive if they lowered their masks. Still, the large majority of health workers seem to endorse corona-fascism.

In April, cities like Nashua, NH once again began to narrow the streets with cement barriers in order to increase the size of restaurants' outdoor seating capacity. Government officials and their Siamese twins in the formerly private sector clearly believe that eating inside of a restaurant will cause everyone in the neighborhood to die.

Masks are now used everywhere, including in ads on billboards and TV.

All around us, there are reminders of the religion of corona-fascism. We are never allowed to go for even a minute without thinking about our new god and his commandments, which we'll get to later.

Google Translate and many other websites attack us with pop-ups about corona-fascism if we ever type in a relevant word. Stores constantly remind us that the virus may be right around the corner, waiting to infect us and kill our families. Children are continually being scared by the rampant paranoia around them.

The majority of people walking outside alone still wear masks.

Many people are still wearing masks while driving alone in cars and while exercising at the gym. Many people still back up when a person gets within six feet during a conversation. The paranoia remains strong after more than a year of corona-fascism.

Children still cannot socialize. Adults still can't go to church or have parties. Holidays are canceled indefinitely. Yes, the 2020 Christmas celebrations throughout the united states were largely canceled.

Virtue signaling is as strong as ever. Politicians and sheep proudly post pictures of themselves with their masks, demonstrating to the world how pious they are. The newly elected Maine Speaker of the House proudly tweeted a picture of the wall of Speakers, of which his portrait was the newest addition. In his photo, he proudly sported the seal of the ultimate religion: corona-fascism. And the comments on his tweet were very supportive of his decision to proudly display his faith.

People are missing check-ups and preventative medicine appointments, causing cancer and other diseases to cause much more harm than necessary.

Sports are still not back to normal, neither youth sports nor professional sports. Despite millions of Americans having acquired immunity to the virus from contracting and defeating it and millions more being vaccinated, sports stadiums remain mostly empty during games, with capacity limited to something like 10% or 20%. They do not allow more than a few fans, because they need their stadiums to look like the new normal, not the reckless old normal, where dirty deplorables drank beer and sat on top of one another while cursing at football players. No, we will never go back to those days. The elites who run the professional sports leagues couldn't let that happen.

Will things get better or worse over the next few months (while this book is in the publishing process)?

It's anyone's guess.

If I had to make a prediction, I'd say that corona-fascism will still be alive and well by June. As I explain in the book, our brilliant overlords and their useful idiots in the private sector are very effective at shifting gears, moving the goalposts, and terrorizing individuals, with brute force if necessary.

While reading this book, please keep these questions in your mind: if the most contagious and deadly virus were raging through the united states for a year and a half, shouldn't everyone be dead by now? At the very least, shouldn't people who refuse to observe mask mandates and social distancing guidelines be dead by now? Why were no hospitals ever overwhelmed? Why were there no bodies in the streets? Why do politicians consistently violate their own safety guidelines if they truly believe that COVID is the most dangerous disease in human history?

Regardless of whether COVID is the most dangerous virus in history, I still do not believe that individual liberties and natural rights should be violated by politicians and police. The only time that I would support the use of force is in self-defense against a person who presents a *clear and present danger* to you. An example of such a danger would be a person holding a gun to your head. A person having a virus is not a clear and present danger.

Because I prioritize natural human rights above everything else, I do not need to prove that COVID is a mild virus that barely killed any people in order to make my point. In fact, I am arguing that COVID could kill 7 billion people in a single day, and I would still not support the elimination of natural rights by politicians. If we allow politicians to justify violating our rights for any reason whatsoever, and if we grant them the authority to determine the legitimacy of that justification, we are conceding that we have zero freedom and that politicians have complete power over us.

In all of my years in medicine and politics, the world's response to this manifestly mild virus is the single most unbelievable thing that I have ever witnessed in my life. It boggles my mind on so many levels, as I will explain throughout this book.

This book is for those who believe in freedom, not dictatorship or any form of authoritarianism. If you believe that you own yourself and your property, you will appreciate this book. If you believe that politicians should not have total control over every single aspect of your life, you will appreciate this book. If you believe that science and data do matter, and if you realize that politicians are sometimes untrustworthy, you are ready to read this book.

Chapter 1

BEFORE CORONA-FASCISM

WHAT DID THE WORLD LOOK like before the pandemic and the accompanying "new normal"? Before the winter of 2019, individuals in the united states and the world had very little personal liberty. As I explain in part one of "The Blueprint For Liberty," we were not nearly as free as we convinced ourselves we were. We were slaves or prisoners with a big yard to roam around in, and ample time to exercise and socialize. But we were still in prison.

Even before corona-fascism, Americans had limited free speech, limited property rights, little to no gun rights (depending on the state), limited due process, limited medical rights, limited educational rights, and diminishing privacy. The 100 or so different taxes combined allowed politicians to steal around 50% of our income. Economic regulations imposed by our masters cost more than 2 trillion dollars in economic productivity each year. Our brilliant lords insist that they must confiscate our money because they know how to spend it much more wisely than we ever could. Never mind the 28 trillion dollars of debt they've accrued. They are still totally fiscally responsible. They promise.

During the time period that may actually come to be known by historians as "B.C.," humans from Wyoming to China and everywhere in between had nearly no privacy or freedom. If we are being honest with ourselves, we must admit that our masters in DC and Silicon Valley can likely see, hear, and track every single thing we do and say and every location we visit. If you check your Google Maps, you will see that Google knows your exact location and can tell you exactly where you were at any point in time. I stumbled upon this Orwellian — albeit convenient — feature after a massive cross-country road trip. Google accurately told me exactly which gas stations we stopped at in each state, including New Mexico, South Dakota, Kentucky, and everywhere else we traveled. If Google knows it, politicians and law enforcement know it. Especially if they ask Google, obtain a warrant, get a subpoena, or hack into our accounts.

Of course, anti-freedom institutions (which describes 99.9% of the institutions in the united states and the world) enthusiastically give politicians any information that could hurt conservatives or the liberty movement without even being asked.[1]

Before corona-fascism, the united states was already moving rapidly toward leftist authoritarian socialism. The polarization within our "country" was already boiling over, sometimes causing actual violence between the right and the left.

While we have been very polarized, it seems like the majority of Americans have long supported authoritarianism in many aspects of daily life. Most Americans support at least some amount of gun control. Most Americans support the government having near total control over healthcare. Most Americans support government control of the economy. Americans support taxation (though they argue bitterly about whether politicians should steal 33% or 34% of our income). Americans consistently elect leaders who spy on them, wage war in literally every country on Earth, and run up a debt of $28 trillion and counting.

The united states were far from perfect before corona, but corona-fascism did bring about a humongous wave of tyranny that changed the world forever.

Chapter 2

THE ORIGIN OF COVID-19

AS OF THIS WRITING, IT is not yet totally confirmed how COVID-19 came into existence and spread among humans. The consensus seems to be that it was created in a lab in Wuhan, China. Many people believe the virus was manipulated by scientists. Some believe it was a natural adaptation of the coronavirus. There are still multiple theories[2] regarding its origin. Due to politicians and their cronies in big tech, it is now unacceptable to question where or how the virus originated, and it is heresy[3] to question[4] any official corona-fascism statement made by our overlords.

Before discussing the origin and spread of the virus, it's important to understand a little bit about politics, especially in China. Even more so than in the united states, the government of China has supreme control over everything. Whatever they say becomes the truth. Dissent is tolerated in China even less than it is in the united states. Xi Jinping is a vicious tyrant who is the leader of the Chinese Communist Party and the dictator of China. No politicians should be trusted. Heads of state should be trusted even less. And world leaders like Xi, Putin, and

Biden should be trusted least of all. Due to his one billion subjects, world-leading economy, top-tier military, amazing espionage, and cyber-warfare operations, Xi is currently the most powerful man on Earth, in my opinion.

In December of 2019, news of the first human transmission of the virus began to spread throughout the world. While doctors are generally very comfortable treating viruses, the coronavirus did present a new challenge for the medical community.

Coronavirus is a family of viruses. Influenza is another family, which is far more common in humans. Coronaviruses very rarely cause humans to become severely sick. This family of viruses generally spreads among animals. Rarely does it mutate into a form that could infect humans and make them sick. It happened once with SARS, and once with MERS, both of which caused major panic within the medical community.

Many doctors practicing now were not around during the last human coronavirus spread. Understandably, this made them very uncomfortable. Politicians around the world sensed the medical community's lack of confidence and grave concern about the virus, so they seized the opportunity to run with it. Thus, corona-paranoia was born.

Chapter 3

ARE THEY INFLATING THE STATISTICS?

I KNOW IT SOUNDS CRAZY to question the united states government in the face of its stellar reputation[5] for accuracy, morality, and consistent principles. It's especially unpopular to question agencies such as the FDA[6] or CDC[7]. However, I have seen so much disturbing evidence that politicians are willfully deceiving us to achieve an agenda that I cannot remain silent.

For the past few months, the united states government has been inflating numbers and exaggerating both the infectiousness and the lethality of COVID-19 (AKA Wuhan Virus). From the beginning of 2020, this whole "pandemic" really did not sit right with me. The government and their naive sheep were acting as if COVID-19 was a super-bug that was 28 trillion times more deadly than "AIDS-Ebola-SARS" and infinitely more contagious than anything humans have ever encountered. Due to the government-media matrix scaring people, many of my friends and relatives began to worry that, if they breathe the same air that an infected person breathed anywhere on Earth, they had a 100% chance of contracting the virus and a 100% chance of dying from it.

If you ask a government official, he or she will generally tell you that this virus is by far the greatest threat to humanity in the history of the universe. This is very far from the truth, though.

While naive and frightened people who listen to everything politicians tell them constantly repeat the phrase that *"this is nothing like the flu,"* I could not really articulate anything that would suggest that they are very different. The primary difference is that the seasonal "flu" is in the family of viruses called "influenza" and COVID-19 is in the family of viruses called "coronaviruses." The flu does seem to infect and kill more children than COVID, but we'll discuss that in depth later.

Many types and subtypes of viruses exist. Many of those affect humans. Of those viruses that affect humans, many manifest as respiratory infections, commonly referred to as a "cold" because it may make you feel congested, give you a cough, make you feel lethargic, and give you a fever. Yes, coronaviruses can cause a common cold, and they may have already been responsible for your cold[8] during the 2019 winter. Much like seasonal influenza viruses, COVID-19 seems to be moderately contagious. Each winter, all of my colleagues and I put on masks for all suspected or confirmed flu contacts. We understand the flu is contagious enough to infect us. We know that it's unlikely to kill us, but we also know that we could easily spread it to our sick and old patients, who could succumb to even a mild virus.

Each year, the seasonal flu kills as many as 80,000 Americans, most of whom are old and/or very sick. I could contend that the flu is considerably more contagious, having infected some 40,000,000+ Americans[9] last season. This is very similar to the behavior and statistics of COVID-19, right?

Dr. Fauci, the doctor in charge of the united states government's COVID-19 response, explains that anyone who has tested positive for

COVID-19 who then dies will be presumed to have died from the virus, even if they were sick prior to the pandemic, even if they had a heart attack or a massive hole from 00 buck shot in their chests.

One frustrated respiratory therapist spoke up about the political pressure on his facility: *"They were calling everything a Covid death… even if it was cancer or natural causes…"*

On April 9th, a doctor from Minnesota went public[10] with the new CDC guidelines. The CDC told doctors throughout the united states that: *"In cases where a definite diagnosis of COVID cannot be made but is suspected or likely, it is acceptable to report COVID-19 on a death certificate as 'probable' or 'presumed.'"*

This is especially peculiar, explained the doctor of 35 years, because *"I've never been encouraged to [notate 'influenza'].... I would probably write 'respiratory arrest' to be the top line, and the underlying cause of this disease would be pneumonia.... I might well put emphysema or congestive heart failure, but I would never put influenza down as the underlying cause of death and yet that's what we are being asked to do here."*

The Texas Dept. of Health recently posted a video[11] of a meeting concerning the pandemic. The government officials in the video explain that the newest guidelines will be even more inclusive and broad than any previous guidelines anywhere in the united states. The person in charge clearly wants every death in the united states to be attributed to COVID.

Two members of The Liberty Block's editorial team have worked in several COVID-dedicated facilities and reported identical guidelines, which state that ANY patient who was declared dead at the facility would have COVID listed as the cause of death, no matter what, and that no autopsy would be performed.

INFECTION FATALITY RATIO
IF INFECTED

0-19 YEARS	.00003%
20-49 YEARS	.0002%
50-69 YEARS	.005%
70+ YEARS	.054%

CDC.GOV

FOX NEWS channel

STATISTICS THE ELITES
DON'T WANT YOU TO SEE

So, the thousands of deaths listed officially as "COVID-19" throughout the united states may have included countless deaths due to the seasonal influenza virus or other illnesses or injuries. Now that the government has lost even more credibility, why should we believe any of their numbers?

As of this writing, there have been 124 million infections and 2.7 million deaths globally, according to Johns Hopkins University.[12] The same dashboard currently says that the united states have had 30 million infections and 500,000 deaths. Of course, those figures are incredibly inflated, as explained above. Further proving how ridiculous this sham is, total deaths from all causes in the united states shows essentially no spike[13] in 2020. This means that all other causes stopped killing people (like the flu,[14] which strangely disappeared[15] in 2020), or that deaths caused by heart disease, cancer, and COPD were misattributed to COVID. An author at Johns Hopkins published an excellent article[16] showing that the data demonstrated that the number of total deaths has remained relatively unaffected in 2020, but they retracted[17] that article once they realized that it severely undermined corona-fascism.

This is so important that it bears repeating:

> ***There was no significant increase in the total number of deaths in the united states in 2020 compared to 2019.***

How could corona-fascism still thrive once people are aware of this?

The guidelines constantly seem to be changing, generally becoming even more broad and ridiculous. Now, any patient who even exhibits any signs commonly associated with any infection (fever, cough, weakness, headache, nausea, diarrhea, tachycardia, bradycardia, difficulty breathing, pain, or any other symptom) is considered to have died of COVID on a death certificate, even if they never had a positive test. The government also wants doctors to list COVID as the cause of death for patients who may have been in contact with a person who was COVID positive or who had any of the above symptoms. Whatever the illness, history, or cause of death, nearly every patient who dies in a hospital has one of the above symptoms during their hospital stay — before dying, of course.

When I first heard about the newest guidelines, I said something along the lines of: *"...fever, rapid heart rate, weakness, difficulty breathing, nausea, diarrhea, pain, chills...but that's like...every patient in every hospital on Earth."*

Exactly.

Chapter 4

THINK OF THE CHILDREN!

ONE OF THE FOUNDATIONS OF a politician's playbook is "*argumenta puerorum*," or the "argument of the children." Control freaks often exclaim that we must ban certain substances or behaviors because such policies could potentially save the life[18] of even one child, which would make it all worthwhile.

Since the beginning of corona-fascism, our masters have been telling us that children are dropping like flies because of COVID, and we must shut down schools and terminate all other socialization, even among children. But are children really vulnerable to the virus?

As it turns out, children are at an even lower risk from the virus than the average person. Children rarely ever contract the virus,[19] they rarely get severely ill[20] if they do contract the virus, and they rarely ever spread[21] the virus to others.[22] This should be cause for optimism, and it should guide policymakers to allow children to socialize. But that is not what happened.

What do the statistics show?

According to the best available data I could find, **around 100-250**

children died from COVID in the united states in 2020. This takes into account the tremendously inflated statistics of coronavirus in the united states. Accurate figures might put child deaths in the teens or single digits.

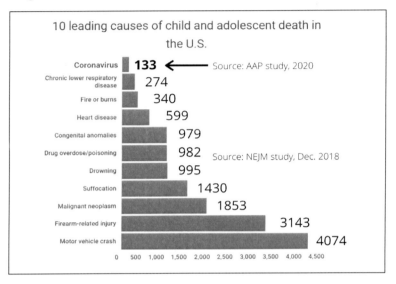

The government of Sweden never closed schools,[23] yet no children died of COVID, and teachers were not negatively affected by the schools remaining open.

The CDC does not seem to publish data on overall deaths of children, though it does have a chart[24] that includes the age groups of under 1, 1-4, 5-9, 10-14, and 15-24. The CDC chart seems to coincide with the NEJM[25] chart included below. The American Academy of Pediatrics (a pro-lockdown, authoritarian association) said that the total number of COVID deaths among children throughout the whole pandemic is 133, as reported by NBC[26] in November. The highest estimate I found comes from a chart from the AAP,[27] which estimates that a total of 241 children have died with COVID from the beginning of the pandemic through February 11th of 2021.

The flu killed 188 children in each of the past two years (the 2018 and 2019 flu seasons), according to the CDC.[28] This is substantially more than COVID, which killed around 100 children in 2020, taking into account massive over-counting. As an experienced advanced-level healthcare provider, it boggles my mind that children are being harmed with masks, quarantine, and other forms of psychological torture due to the threat of COVID, but no such precautions were even considered due to the flu. Massive amounts of data have demonstrated that while children are susceptible to contracting, spreading, and suffering severe illness from the flu, they rarely contract COVID, nearly never[29] spread it, and essentially never become severely ill from it. Furthermore, considering that the coronavirus replaced the flu[30] in 2020, children are literally safer than ever before. For the first time in recent history, they could be children without even worrying about the flu. We should be celebrating that and letting them live life. We should not be traumatizing them and scarring them for life.

However, politicians and their loyal and paranoid followers are destroying their children's mental (and physical) health by locking them inside, keeping them from friends and normal activities, and brainwashing them with intense paranoia, convincing them that they will die horrible deaths if they even lower their masks for an instant. What is the result of this? We are beginning to see that children[31] and adults are becoming depressed,[32] turning to drugs,[33] and killing themselves at alarming rates,[34] not to mention the child abuse[35] and domestic violence[36] fueled by corona-fascism.

According to the New England Journal of Medicine[37] and the CDC,[38] fires kill around three times as many children as COVID, choking kills around fourteen times as many children as COVID, drowning kills around nine times as many children as COVID, heart disease kills around six times as many children as COVID, cancer kills around eighteen times as many children as COVID, suicide kills eleven times more children than COVID, homicide kills eighteen times as many children as COVID, and poisoning kills around eight times as many children as COVID.

Needless to say, COVID would not make the top-ten list of causes of deaths for children in the united states If society must totally restructure everything in existence to save 100 children in the united states per year, it certainly must criminalize fires and hot water, ban all dangerous substances, abolish all firearms, and prohibit the use of pools and require all children to wear flotation devices at all times, lest they drown.

Especially when discussing pediatric immunology, we must at least touch on the basic concept known as the "hygiene hypothesis."[39] Over the past few decades, western medicine,[40] and specifically doctors specializing in immunology and infectious diseases, have reached a consensus, meaning that it's not just a hypothesis anymore. The data shows that children who are not exposed to pathogens (viruses and bacteria) and/or children who are drowned in hand sanitizer and anti-bacterial soap do not properly develop immune systems. This is hardly shocking, because we all learned in middle school that humans generally achieve immunity to a given pathogen by being exposed to it (or a vaccine or a similar pathogen). While it may not be wise to purposely expose your baby to every single pathogen in the universe in one day, going too far in the other direction – sanitizing your child's developing immune system — is certainly harmful.

In September of 2019, US News advised readers to ensure that their immune systems develop properly, recommending to "Reduce your use of chlorine-based cleaners, skip the antibacterial soaps, start a garden, consider getting a pet, and to have closer interactions with people."

In 2017, the Independent[41] published an article about immunology, quoting Professor Gilbert, the director of the Microbiome Center at the University of Chicago:[42]

> "...parents can often over-sterilize environments for their children. When children are in the garden playing in mud, for example, it's not necessary to immediately sterilize their hands and worry that the mud may have got close to their faces.... The fear that children should be kept out of contact with animals because of germs is also unfounded, according to Prof Gilbert. Instances such as a dog licking a child's face are in fact beneficial for their immune system rather than a cause for concern."

There is certainly a healthy balance between living life in a paranoid, super-sanitized manner with no exposure to any molecule in existence and sending your children to African jungles without any shots. It is disappointing to me that the rest of the medical (or political?) community seems silent about this balance now that we are living in a "new normal," where pathogens, medicine, data, and logic no longer factor into public policy.

Considering that children are unlikely to contract the coronavirus, unlikely to spread it (especially if asymptomatic), and unlikely to be severely affected by it, politicians and parents ought to reconsider whether the cost of the "new normal" is worth the damage. Society is severely harming[43] children in so many ways, and the maximum possible benefit of totally eliminating COVID would spare around 100 children from death, according to the best available data. If we are to flip the world upside down for anything that kills over 100 children per year, we must make some radical changes to stop the hundreds of deaths from drowning, fires, cancer, heart disease, and the many other ailments that kill far more children than the coronavirus.

Instead of allowing children to live their lives, our lords closed their schools in the middle of the year, covered their faces, and prohibited them from seeing their friends. How much more evil could politicians be?

Chapter 5

MASKING OVER HUMANITY

WHAT MAKES US HUMAN?

Among the most important differences between animals and humans is our ability to communicate on a much deeper level than animals. Humans are capable of profound communication because of our human brains, faces, and speech. Masks have an effect on all factors involved in communication.

Scientists agree that 70 to 93 percent[44] of communication is non-verbal. Facial expressions are perpetually communicating our emotions to others, both consciously and unconsciously. If humans did not have faces, a tremendous part of their humanity and ability to communicate would be lost. Nearly all humor is accompanied by a smile. Without a smile, humorous comments are often perceived by the listener as offensive. This has happened to me quite a bit over the past year, thanks to masks.

Over the past year, our lords, their royal enforcers, and their media allies have covered our faces. The general recommendation from our masters is to wear masks whenever around others, even when at home,[45] in a car,[46] exercising,[47] and between bites[48] while eating.

The result of the mask mandates, which were implemented in nearly every state and country on Earth, has been terribly damaging. Communication between people has been substantially harmed.

When seconds matter, clear communication could literally be the difference between life and death.

In emergency medicine, I have witnessed firsthand how miscommunication could negatively affect patients.

"Give her 15 of fentanyl, please."

"Okay, Doc, I'll give her 50 of fentanyl as soon as I finish with this report."

Of course, these miscommunications happen plenty without masks. But add masks to the equation, and words become so muffled that errors with medications, treatments, and diagnoses can happen much more often.

Air traffic control has also become more dangerous because of the "religion of the mask." When pilots communicate with air traffic control on the ground, the quality of the communication is already very poor. Radios simply do not have high audio quality, and there is no facial or non-verbal communication between pilots and ground officials, of course. When Biden forced air traffic control employees on the ground to wear masks[49] while speaking to pilots over the radio, he may have compromised the safety of pilots and airplane passengers by making communication even more difficult. Even one muffled message that is misinterpreted or that must be repeated could make a world of difference when airplanes are traveling at 500 mph. The concerns about muffled communication by the air traffic control whistleblower were confirmed by a pilot[50] shortly afterward, who complained that the poor communication due to masks was a real hazard. Still, the priests of the "religion of the mask" insist that wearing a mask is the most noble thing a human can do. As with many religions, its most zealous observers believe that it is worth dying for.

On a more personal level, the masks have certainly harmed many people, too. Much like they do with regard to the harm to the economy, coronavirus zealous dismiss concerns of dating being destroyed by the corona-paranoia. However, much like the economy, life would hardly exist without dating.

For those who are not totally familiar with the biological conception of a baby, let me explain: Babies are generally conceived by a man and a woman who get together, date for a while, often get married, and have sex. Before they fall in love and get married and begin to have children, they generally spend time with each other. This is called "dating." Before 2020, men and women used to date each other. We used to flirt with each other quite often. Before meeting my wife in 2015, I dated numerous women and I flirted with many more. Very often, the first conversation was preceded by a glance and a smile at each other. Countless relationships began with a smile. In fact, many readers of this book were likely born because their parents shared a smile.

A meta-analysis of 138 global studies[51] on smiling found that it has a positive impact on happiness. Smiling at one another makes both parties happier, less stressed, boosts confidence, and improves immunity[52] (ironic, isn't it?).

But the dating scene is not just handicapped by the masks blocking most of the potential partner's face. The social conditioning — er, social distancing guidelines have caused nearly every person to avoid others. It's pretty difficult to talk or flirt with a prospective partner if you must "maintain a distance of at least six feet from other people at all times." I am not even talking about getting to first or second base; young adults haven't been allowed to get off of home plate since 2019. Thank God I am already happily married. If I were still dating during this government-imposed dating halt, I would be quite frustrated.

Much like smiling, the total lack of dating and relationships is taking a toll on mental health. Is that just my hypothesis? Well, Dr. Robert Redfield, the director of the CDC[53] said a few months ago that:

> *"We're seeing, sadly, far greater suicides now than we are deaths from COVID. We're seeing far greater deaths from drug overdose that are above excess that we had as background than we are seeing the deaths from COVID."*

At the time of this writing, in March of 2021, nearly everyone in the united states seems to be afraid to be near any other person. They have been brainwashed to believe that everyone is infected with the virus. They believe they have a 100% chance of catching the virus. They believe that, if they contract the virus, they have a 100% chance of dying. They even believe this is the case among children, which we debunked in the last chapter. This paranoia takes a heavy psychological toll on individuals.

What do anxious, depressed, lonely teenage girls need when they think matters couldn't possibly get worse? Acne!

In addition to all of the other negative effects of masks on our social lives and mental health, wearing a mask all of the time causes a massive buildup of oils and dirt on the skin, which causes terrible pimple breakouts[54] on the face. At least the teenagers with no social life and lots of pimples and sadness could have lots of time at home reading about how masks don't actually protect the wearer from COVID-19.[55]

Tremendous amounts of data refute the bogus theory that masks could stop a respiratory illness. Here are just a few of the published medical and scientific studies proving this point:

Jacobs, J.L. et al. (2009) "Use of surgical face masks to reduce the incidence of the common cold among health care workers in Japan: A randomized controlled trial," American Journal of Infection Control,[56] Volume 37, Issue 5, 417-419.

"N95-masked health-care workers (HCW) were significantly more likely to experience headaches. Face mask use in HCW was not demonstrated to provide benefit in terms of cold symptoms or getting colds."

Cowling, B. et al. (2010) "Face masks to prevent transmission of influenza virus: A systematic review," Epidemiology and Infection,[57] 138(4), 449-456.

"None of the studies reviewed showed a benefit from wearing a mask, in either HCW or community members in households (H)."

bin-Reza et al. (2012) "The use of masks and respirators to prevent transmission of influenza: a systematic review of the scientific evidence," Influenza and Other Respiratory Viruses,[58] (4), 257–267.

"There were 17 eligible studies.... None of the studies established a conclusive relationship between mask/respirator use and protection against influenza infection."

Smith, J.D. et al. (2016) "Effectiveness of N95 respirators versus surgical masks in protecting health care workers from acute respiratory infection: a systematic review and meta-analysis," CMAJ[59] Mar 2016.

> *"We identified six clinical studies.... In the meta-analysis of the clinical studies, we found no significant difference between N95 respirators and surgical masks in associated risk of (a) laboratory-confirmed respiratory infection, (b) influenza-like illness, or (c) reported work-place absenteeism."*

Offeddu, V. et al. (2017) "Effectiveness of Masks and Respirators Against Respiratory Infections in Healthcare Workers: A Systematic Review and Meta-Analysis," Clinical Infectious Diseases,[60] Volume 65, Issue 11, 1 December 2017, Pages 1934–1942

> *"Self-reported assessment of clinical outcomes was prone to bias. Evidence of a protective effect of masks or respirators against verified respiratory infection (VRI) was not statistically significant."*

Radonovich, L.J. et al. (2019) "N95 Respirators vs Medical Masks for Preventing Influenza Among Health Care Personnel: A Randomized Clinical Trial," JAMA,[61] 2019; 322(9): 824–833

> *"Among 2,862 randomized participants, 2,371 completed the study and accounted for 5,180 HCW-seasons.... Among outpatient health care personnel, N95 respirators vs medical masks as worn by participants in this trial resulted in no significant difference in the incidence of laboratory-confirmed influenza."*

Long, Y. et al. (2020) "Effectiveness of N95 respirators versus surgical masks against influenza: A systematic review and meta-analysis," J Evid Based Med.[62] 2020; 1- 9.

> *"A total of six RCTs involving 9,171 participants were included. There were no statistically significant differences in preventing laboratory-confirmed influenza, laboratory-confirmed respiratory viral infections, laboratory-confirmed respiratory infection, and influenza-like illness using N95 respirators and surgical masks. Meta-analysis indicated a protective effect of N95 respirators against laboratory-confirmed bacterial colonization (RR = 0.58, 95% CI 0.43-0.78). The use of N95 respirators compared with surgical masks is not associated with a lower risk of laboratory-confirmed influenza."*

Furthermore, states without mask mandates such as South Dakota (and Florida, which has been relatively free of corona-fascism over the past year) have had no worse outcomes by any measurable statistics when compared to states with moderate to severe mask mandates and lockdowns. In fact, the data seems to suggest that mask mandates are correlated with worse COVID rates.[63]

Of course, the virus is roughly as contagious or less so than the flu. It is likely less dangerous than the flu. Furthermore, millions of people have already had the virus, and many more have been vaccinated. The two aforementioned groups have nearly 100% immunity from coronavirus. This means that they cannot contract the virus, which means they could not possibly infect others with the virus. And anyone who does not have active COVID with active symptoms also poses nearly zero risk to others. So why can't at least some of us be allowed to breathe freely?

Why are NFL stadiums strictly limited to a few thousand people when they could easily allow 100,000 people who are immune to COVID and totally healthy — and happily willing to accept the risks of going to the game?

We will address this sociopathic twisted thinking in a later chapter.

Chapter 6

DO MASKS HAVE ANY DOWNSIDE?

ONE OF THE MOST COMMON phrases repeated by corona-fascism zealots is that you should just wear the damned mask because it's only a tiny inconvenience with no downside.

Well…you know what's coming next!

In addition to all of the horrible negative effects on socialization, happiness, safety, and mental health that we discussed in the last chapter, masks have quite a few serious medical effects on people, as well.

Wearing a mask for extended periods of time causes at least some degree of hypoxia (low oxygen level) and some amount of hypercapnia (high carbon dioxide level). This is a topic that I do have nine years of intimate experience with. A very large portion of my critically ill patients were primarily in my ambulance because of an oxygen issue, a CO2 issue, or both. I am well aware of the effect of carbon dioxide and oxygen on the brain, our acid-base balance, and so many other systems within our bodies.

The following describes just a few issues that could be caused by breathing through a mask for extended periods of time.

Unless people use a new mask every single time they put one on their face — and never touch the mask or their face with non-sterile hands — they are not using the mask properly. Masks are uncomfortable, they itch, and they slide down the face. So imperfect humans adjust them. Constantly. Doctors, nurses, paramedics, and EMTs are not totally innocent. In fact, I have found that every health care provider touches his or her mask too often (I plead the 5th on this one).

Because people constantly adjust (read: contaminate) their masks and reuse them for months at a time, the masks may actually be more harmful than helpful. The entire reason for wearing a mask is to prevent pathogens from entering the airway (mouth, nose, trachea, bronchi, alveoli). If we allow pathogens to contaminate the inside surface of a mask, we are giving the dangerous virus a convenient ride right to our mouth, which is the entrance to the airway. As soon as we take the first inhalation with the mask on, the pathogens enter our lungs, where they enjoy an excellent chance of successfully infecting us.

Worse yet, wearing masks may actually help pathogens get deeper into our lungs. Because masks increase resistance and make it harder to breathe in and out, we often take a very deep breath when we inhale with the mask on, especially if we are exerting ourselves and need to move more CO_2 out and oxygen into our lungs. By taking the forceful inhalation, we are bringing the pathogens from the mask deep into our lungs, possibly to the end of the airways (alveoli). If you want instant lung infection (pneumonia), this is a wonderful way to guarantee it!

Could this be a reason why we saw many severe pneumonia[64] cases with COVID?

Common sense and science tell us that masks cause a decrease in oxygen intake and an increase in retained carbon dioxide. Carbon dioxide is the byproduct of cellular metabolism, and is converted to acid in the body. If CO_2 is allowed to accumulate in the body for too long, acidosis could be very harmful, and even lethal. Mild acidosis is still not desirable.

Likewise, if a person cannot obtain enough oxygen, his or her body suffers. The most sensitive organ is the brain. Even slightly low oxygen levels for even short periods of time can cause the brain to suffer. The brain does not regenerate like other parts of the body, so injuries are generally life-long. If a person has a low oxygen level for even a few minutes, he or she could suffer a hypoxic brain injury, which could cause many forms of brain damage. The good news is that healthy people who are awake and oriented will know they are hypoxic before it becomes truly dangerous. But if a person has an oxygen saturation of around 90%, they may feel pretty normal. Such mild hypoxia may only cause a few mild symptoms, which might only begin after a few hours of mild hypoxia. They might feel lethargic, irritable, anxious, and they might have a headache, poor memory, or feel mildly short of breath. Ironically, many people could associate these symptoms with COVID itself, which is very problematic.

Wearing a mask for a few minutes is very unlikely to cause any of these issues, in my opinion. But, for those who spend the majority of their waking hours breathing through a mask (or two masks or an N95), they likely caused some hypoxia and/or hypercapnia (which may also cause some of the above symptoms). Are people going to suffer severe brain damage or become paraplegic from mask-induced mild hypoxia? I can't imagine that happening. But if you are hypoxic or hypercarbic enough to feel any of the above symptoms, I would strongly recommend taking the mask off and breathing normally. Could there be some long-term mild effects such as memory issues from this 15-month episode of mild hypoxia? That data remains to be seen.

As the body remains mildly to moderately hypoxic for a long period of time, our brilliant bodies do make some adjustments. Without getting too deep into the biology, our bone marrow produces red blood cells, which contain hemoglobin, a protein that oxygen binds to in order to hitch a ride around the bloodstream. In an extremely complicated cascade, oxygen molecules are delivered to all of the cells in the body that need it in order to metabolize energy and survive. The hemoglobin (Hgb) are the seats and the red blood cells are the buses that carry oxygen. Anemic patients are always tired because they don't have enough red blood cells, meaning they can't get enough oxygen to their tissues. This is a form of (cellular) hypoxia.

A study[65] published by the National Institute of Health/the government's national library of medicine found that even surgeons were negatively affected by wearing surgical masks, which are much thinner than N95 masks. After just one hour of surgery, the presumably healthy doctors had a significant decrease in arterial oxygen saturation levels, according to the study:

> *"Considering our findings, pulse rates of the surgeons increase and SpO2 decrease after the first hour. This early change in SpO2 may be either due to the facial mask or the operational stress. Since a very small decrease in saturation at this level reflects a large decrease in PaO2, our findings may have a clinical value for the health workers and the surgeons."*

Of course, we didn't need a study to tell us what we all know very well from experience. Wearing a mask (especially an N95 mask) for extended periods and/or during exercise such as walking up stairs, makes us significantly short of breath. I am in elite physical health (boxer, powerlifter, gymnast, runner, etc.) and I become short of breath when walking when I wear an N95 mask.

Healthy bodies adjust to chronically low oxygen levels by simply producing more red blood cells. The kidney synthesizes a hormone called erythropoietin (EPO) which is the messenger that tells the bone marrow to increase RBC production. Technically, more RBCs translates to more potential oxygen-carrying capacity. People who have long-term hypoxia cause their bodies to increase the amount of RBCs via this mechanism. Patients with chronic lung diseases such as COPD have higher levels of RBCs in their blood. People who live at high altitudes develop high levels of RBCs.

While an increased number of red blood cells does allow a person to carry more oxygen (and therefore to have better cardio), there are some risks involved with secondary polycythemia.[66] Due to the blood becoming thicker from the increased percentage of red blood cells, the risk for thromboembolic (clotting) events increases as the RBCs increase. The thicker blood causes an increased likelihood[67] of strokes, heart attacks, pulmonary emboli, DVTs, and other infarct. I do not believe that everyone who puts on a mask will have a polycythemia-induced heart attack or stroke immediately, but public policy must take all potential harmful effects into account before enacting a policy. And I doubt that our overlords thought about any of this for an instant.

While we're on the topic of me working on an ambulance, I think that it's as good a time as any to bring up an awkward but sufficiently relevant issue with working while wearing a mask. Like millions of other providers, I often wear glasses. As everyone who wears glasses learned during corona-fascism, the first exhalation while wearing a mask often fogs up our glasses, totally obstructing our vision. As an experienced driver, you can believe me when I tell you it's pretty important to be able to see while driving. Whenever I wear glasses and a mask while driving, I must choose between seeing the road and obeying the God of medicine, Dr. Anthony Fauci.

The fogged up glasses don't just affect EMTs and paramedics, though. Doctors and nurses who don't drive with patients could also experience difficulties with poor vision. It turns out that doctors can't intubate without seeing, and nurses have trouble starting IVs without seeing the patient's arm. Again, maybe this is something that should at least be considered or discussed by our masters in DC.

Do masks have a negative effect on society at large? Well, only if you have an issue with child sex trafficking.

Each year, as many as 12 million children[68] are trafficked for the primary purpose of sexual abuse. These children might have a chance of being found and rescued, but only if their faces are visible. By normalizing the covering of children's faces, politicians have made life for child traffickers much easier. These sociopathic criminals could hold child sex slaves against their will and even go out in public with them because the chance of the children being recognized is severely diminished due to the child's face being covered.

Chapter 7

EVERYONE IS SICK!

FOR DECADES, CITIZENS IN THE united states have been presumed guilty until they prove their innocence to the government. Despite the standard civics lessons taught in government-operated propaganda schools, once a cop accuses a person of a crime, that person is legally recognized as being guilty. The burden of proof in the corrupt court systems in the united states is on the accused, not on the government.

When you are accused by a cop of running a stop sign, you are given a ticket before you are convicted in court. Without a judge or a jury, the cop has the power to demand your money, and he has a badge and a gun to make sure you obey. You are guilty. If you wish to take the government to court (which is conveniently controlled by the government, conflicts of interest be damned), you can dispute the charge. This would entail taking off from work for at least one day, driving to the court, possibly hiring a lawyer, and then trying to convince a government agent to literally rule against his own coworker and declare that you are not guilty. Even in a best-case scenario, you just lost a lot of money (missed work, travel, legal fees, etc.). This means that even if you were 100% innocent, you still suffered a real material loss — which is a punishment — because a cop determined you were guilty and punished you before you had any sort of due process.[69]

Over the past few months, we have seen this authoritarian phenomenon evolve in a disturbing fashion. Before politicians abolished the concept of freedom, people were free to do as they pleased. They could do anything they desired, as long as they did not harm anyone else or violate another's property. If they did violate another person, the others in the community would stop them, punish them, or demand restitution. They could even do reckless things like breathe without a mask, smoke plants, drive cars, work for a living, and much more.

Once politicians began to take power away from individuals, personal freedom began to diminish. Innocent and peaceful people were increasingly forced to obtain permission from politicians and cops to do normal things like work, drive, and purchase items. When contagious diseases began to spread throughout societies, those who were confirmed to have the disease were relegated to their homes. If a person resisted such orders, government authorities might use force to keep the person in his or her home, claiming that the health of the collective[70] was more important than the personal liberty of the individual.

And then corona-paranoia struck Earth.

Within a few months, power-drunk politicians began to make ridiculous mandates, each of which violated individual liberty in a uniquely harsh manner. State dictators (formerly referred to as "governors") began completely ignoring their legislatures and implemented one order after another. One of the general themes of the dictators' executive orders was that every human alive is presumed to be infected with coronavirus and super-contagious. Never mind that the virus statistics have been inflated[71] as nothing has ever been inflated before (except for maybe the dollar[72]). Never mind that many people are immune to it entirely, especially those who already had the virus. And never mind that children are rarely susceptible, nor are they contagious when they do get the virus. Facts don't matter when we are busy "trusting the experts." Also, never mind[73] that the "experts"[74] are, themselves, corrupt[75] politicians.

Without any input from legislators, dictators in nearly every state declared that all persons were guilty of harboring and spreading the coronavirus. Therefore, every person would have to wear a mask,[76] stay at least six feet away from others, and obey many more ridiculous and authoritarian laws. Businesses were declared guilty of being corona-venues and were shut down or crippled by dictators' regulations. Those who obeyed all of the restrictions and visited restaurants were tracked[77] like Jews in 1940 Germany or slaves on plantations, only with the added dystopian tyranny of modern surveillance technology. Dictators unilaterally granted their vicious enforcers permission to enter any private property[78] without a warrant and punish any individual if they did so for corona-fascist reasons. When individuals who already had the virus asked their dictator or local police if they could breathe without a mask because they now have total immunity to the virus, they were harshly condemned for corona-crimes, the most heinous class of crimes[79] in our post-sensical society.

Dictators have made it clear: You are guilty and you are infected with the coronavirus. If you already had it? You are still guilty and still a potential carrier and spreader, and you must be treated as such. If you received the vaccine, you are still considered to have coronavirus. If you test positive and attempt to go outside, police will violently take you into custody[80] anyway. State legislators — the men and women elected by their constituents to represent them by proposing and voting on legislation — have stood by as their dictators have taken over full legislative control of their states. For this reason, state legislatures are now literally obsolete.[81] Law enforcement has embraced corona-fascism and has gladly enforced the most vicious violations of liberty and humanity since the Third Reich.

There is one key difference between the tyrannical presumption of guilt and the dystopian presumption of illness. In the case of the former, one could at least theoretically prove his or her innocence and be granted relief. In the case of corona-fascism, it is 100% impossible to prove to our dictators and their armed enforcers that we are not infected with the virus. We are all considered to be filthy, sick, guilty slaves, and we are abused by our sociopathic leaders.

Chapter 8

WHAT IS THEIR MOTIVE?

MANY PEOPLE IMMEDIATELY THROW A flag and call "conspiracy" as soon as they hear any claim about people benefiting financially (or otherwise) from the corona-fascism that has consumed the entire Earth. If you have already made up your mind about politicians being angels who would never engage in any corrupt behavior, you will not like this chapter very much, so you can close the book and go back to your leftist activism on Facebook or Twitter. If you believe in evidence and logic, read on.

WHO MADE MONEY FROM CORONA-FASCISM?

Hospitals

For at least a few months, and possibly since the very beginning of the outbreak, politicians have been using taxpayer dollars to incentivize hospitals to inflate[82] the amount of COVID cases, hospitalizations, ventilator usage, and deaths. Politicians in DC have been giving the hospitals $13,000[83] in exchange for each "diagnosis," even if an actual COVID test was never performed. If a patient was placed on a ventilator due to "COVID," the federal government gave the hospital $39,000.[84] So ask yourself what you'd expect hospital administrators and doctors to do if they were offered huge sums of money each time they said the word "coronavirus."

Politicians and Their Cronies

The united states government is also giving states billions of tax-payer dollars. How much each state receives seems to depend on its population and how severe the outbreak appears to be in their state.

For example: Being a good statesman, Dictator Sununu is making New Hampshire seem as sick as possible so that Trump sends him as much money as possible. It's understandable why Sununu would shut down the state's economy for months on end. I can assume from his actions that he wanted billions of dollars for his state budget so that he could cut taxes or not increase taxes or cut spending. Additionally, he certainly did not want to be responsible for a worsening pandemic outbreak in his state, so he wanted to play it safe. Taking away some freedom is much less politically damaging than fueling a pandemic.

The sociopaths from DC have benefited from the virus in multiple ways. Firstly, they took away massive amounts of our liberty and gave it to themselves in the form of power. The amount of freedom we have lost since 2019 cannot be overstated. It was tremendous, and our lives will never be the same because of it. Secondly, they were able to enrich[85] many of their allies[86] in the united states and around the world by granting them massive government contracts and by giving them billions of dollars with each "COVID stimulus"[87] bill. Among the recipients of taxpayer dollars via the government's "Paycheck Protection Program" were Speaker of the House Nancy Pelosi's husband and Senate Majority Leader Mitch McConnell's wife, each of whom may have received as much as a million dollars.[88] Keep in mind that all this money was initially taken from people like you and me via taxation.

Additionally, many politicians used highly unethical information to make huge gains by buying and selling[89] the right stocks at the right time, allowing them to benefit handsomely from corona-induced market volatility.

This same corrupt cronyism[90] occurred in Britain,[91] too. I'm sure it occurs in every state on Earth that is unfortunate enough to be ruled by politicians.

Every company that manufactures or sells gloves, masks, gowns, face shields, plexiglass, and many other items that have now become part of everyone's lives likely made out like bandits due to the billions of taxpayer dollars being funneled to them by governments. They also likely made billions from private companies purchasing such supplies due to political and societal pressures.

Somewhat related to the above cronyism is the concept of "competition elimination." Politicians destroyed many small businesses with regulations those small businesses could not handle, or by simply passing laws forcing them to shut their doors. This paved a clear path for the huge retailers such as Amazon and Walmart, whose owners are surely in bed with politicians. Why do you think Walmart supported corona-fascism so much? It helped eliminate their competition, of course.

In 2020, Walmart[92] donated $5 million to politicians and spent $6.4 million on lobbying politicians.

In 2020, Amazon[93] donated $12.8 million to politicians and spent $18.7 million lobbying politicians. The company donated $2 million to Biden, around a million dollars to the DNC, and almost a million dollars to Bernie Sanders during the year of the pandemic.

If you're interested in learning more about which "private" businesses own politicians, you may find OpenSecrets.org very interesting.

As far as individual companies that are traded on the stock market, here is how a few of them did during the pandemic:

- Zoom (which seems disturbingly loyal to the CCP[94]) quadrupled during COVID.

- Microsoft nearly doubled during COVID.

- Amazon nearly doubled during COVID.

- China benefited by crippling the western economy, improving its position among world leaders to the number one spot. They also likely made billions of dollars[95] by selling ridiculous amounts of masks, gloves, and other supplies to the rest of the world for the past year.

All of this amounts to one very important discovery, which is critical to proving any criminal act: **motive**. The politicians and their cronies had incredible amounts of powerful motives to conduct what may be the biggest assault on personal liberty in world history, except for actual genocides.

As spin experts, the Biden administration has continued to use COVID as justification for many more harmful policies.

After four years of condemning Trump's handling of immigration and border policies, Biden has not changed much at the border in his first few months as president. In fact, Biden is still locking children in cages. Construction of the border wall was halted once Trump left office, and Democrats have promised to dismantle what was built. With less border security, massive amounts of unvetted illegal immigrants have been flooding into the united states. Immigrants all over the world have received the message that we are opening our borders for anyone who wants to enter. Still, the conditions within the facilities at the border that contain some immigrants are in horrific condition. When asked why they will not let the media report on the facilities, Biden's DHS secretary, Alejandro Mayorkas[96] blamed COVID. He said the press can't get close to the immigration facilities because they would get COVID if they took photos or videos to report to the American people.

Mayorkas also assured Chris Wallace the Biden administration will release some government-approved video footage to the media soon.

Have no fear, though. Project Veritas did obtain a leaked photo[97] of one of the facilities. You can only hide the truth for so long.

We can now know with total certainty that politicians will continue to use COVID as their go-to whenever they need to justify doing anything. If something occurs and the politicians want to take away our liberties or our money, all they need to do is mention COVID. It's the new 9/11. It is a joker that can be plugged into any situation, and it cannot be argued against.

In fact, 12 socialist members of Congress recently proposed a bill that would give every American over the age of 16 who earns less than $130,000/year $2,000 each month until the pandemic is over (which I still think means every month for eternity). H.R. 6553[98] would also include $1,000 checks each month for another year after the pandemic is over. Undocumented immigrants would also receive this monthly universal basic income,[99] funded by taxpayers like you and me.

What is their justification for the bill? Coronavirus, of course!

Chapter 9

ECONOMIC DEVASTATION

ONE OF THE MOST HORRIBLE effects of corona-fascism was the crippling of the world's economy. Due to fear-porn being created and circulated around the world at unimaginable levels by politicians, the stock market crashed on March 9th, causing a worldwide recession.

The Dow Jones Industrial Average (an index consisting of the 30 largest publicly traded American companies) plummeted by 2,000 points, which was 7.8%. This was the biggest single-day drop in history. A few days later, the DJIA dropped 2,300 points in a day. A few days after that, it dropped 3,000 points, which is now the single worst day[100] in the DJIA's history. When the S&P 500 (the 500 largest publicly traded American companies) plummeted by 7.2% in the first 15 minutes of trading, a Level-1 circuit breaker was triggered, which halted trading. This saved the market from falling even further. Still, by March 23, the index would lose 34% of its value.[101] All in all, the corona-crash was one of the worst market downturns in the united states and in world history.

"So what? A few evil billionaires lost some of their money. Who cares?! That is nothing compared to the many lives saved by the lockdowns and other restrictions on the economy, right?"

Wrong. Oh, so very, very wrong.

Firstly, nearly every person in the united states and the world has money in the markets or is at least affected by the stock market. If you have any investments, a 401(k), other pension plans, an IRA, mutual funds, or other investments, your money is either in the market or affected by the market. Technically, every asset in existence is affected by the stock market (though many commodities have an inverse relationship with the stock market).

Secondly, your employer, your restaurant, your relatives, your neighbors, your friends, your government, your local economy, and your tax base are almost certainly invested in the stock market.

As the stock market crashes, people panic. They do not shop. When commerce ceases, businesses go bankrupt. When businesses fail, employees lose their jobs. Without any jobs, the rest of your community loses their homes.

Are you starting to get the picture?

Economic collapse *is* societal collapse.

Prosperity *is* health.

In fact, the less money individuals have, the shorter their life expectancy.

But don't take my word for it. Look at all the statistics on life expectancy in the world, separated by state, class, or any other metric. Then look into individual incomes around the world. I did a bit of that research for you, and the data can be found in the two graphics below. The first chart shows life expectancy rates, and the second image is a study proving the link between income and life expectancy.

REGION RANK	LIFEX	WORLD RANK	REGION RANK	LIFEX	WORLD RANK
1. Mauritius	74.82	82	26. Zambia	62.33	160
2. Seychelles	73.26	93	27. Gambia	61.92	161
3. Cape Verde	73.17	96	28. Zimbabwe	61.45	162
4. Sao Tome	68.72	126	29. Benin	61.09	163
5. Rwanda	68.04	129	30. Togo	60.61	164
6. Senegal	66.77	161	31. DR Congo	60.45	165
7. Kenya	66.68	132	32. Burkina Faso	60.32	166
8. Gabon	66.45	134	33. Mozambique	30.10	167
9. Madagascar	66.09	137	34. Burundi	30.10	168
10. Botswana	68.05	138	35. Guinea-Bissau	59.83	169
11. Ethiopia	65.51	141	36. Niger	59.83	170
12. Sudan	65.12	143	37. Guinea	59.80	171
13. Eritrea	64.97	144	38. Equ. Guinea	59.54	172
14. Congo	64.30	145	39. South Sudan	58.65	173
15. Malawi	64.17	146	40. Cameroon	58.06	174
16. Mauritania	63.94	147	41. Mali	57.95	175
17. Tanzania	63.91	148	42. Swaziland	57.69	176
18. Comoros	63.86	149	43. Somalia	55.45	177
19. Djibouti	63.84	150	44. Nigeria	55.19	178
20. Namibia	63.68	152	45. Cote d Ivoire	54.59	178
21. South Africa	63.60	153	46. Chad	54.26	180
22. Ghana	63.45	155	47. Sierra Leone	53.13	181
23. Liberia	62.94	156	48. Central Africa	53.04	182
24. Angola	62.63	158	49. Lesotho	52.94	183
25. Uganda	62.50	159			

Results The sample consisted of 1 408 287 218 person-year observations (mean age at which individuals were analyzed, 53.0 years; median household earnings among working individuals, $61 175 per year [mean, $97 725 per year]). Among those aged 40 to 76 years, there were 4 114 380 deaths among men (mortality rate, 596.3 per 100 000) and 2 694 808 deaths among women (mortality rate, 375.1 per 100 000). The analysis yielded four results. First, higher income was associated with greater longevity throughout the income distribution. The gap in life expectancy between the richest 1% and poorest 1% of individuals was 14.6 years (95% CI, 14.4 to 14.8 years) for men and 10.1 years (95% CI, 9.9 to 10.3 years) for women. Second, inequality in life expectancy increased over time. Between 2001 and 2014, life expectancy increased by 2.34 years for men and 2.91 years for women in the top 5% of the income distribution, but increased by only 0.32 years for men and 0.04 years for women in the bottom 5% ($P< .001$ for the difference for both sexes). Third, life expectancy varied substantially across local areas. For individuals in the bottom income quartile, life expectancy differed by approximately 4.5 years between areas with the highest and lowest longevity. Changes in life expectancy between 2001 and 2014 ranged from gains of more than 4 years to losses of more than 2 years across areas. Fourth, geographic differences in life expectancy for individuals in the lowest income quartile were significantly correlated with health behaviors such as smoking ($r = -0.69$, $P< .001$), but were not significantly correlated with access to medical care, physical environmental factors, income inequality, or labor market conditions. Life expectancy for low income individuals was positively correlated with the local area fraction of immigrants ($r = 0.72$, $P < .001$), fraction of college graduates ($r = 0.42$, $P< .001$), and local government expenditures ($r = 0.57$, $P < .001$).
Credit: JAMA. 2016;315(16):1750-1766. doi:10.1001/jama.2016.4226

Additionally, economic depressions cause emotional depression — and lots of suicides and drug use. The market crash of 2008 may have been responsible for over 10,000 suicides.[102] The market crash caused by politicians in 2020 could be exponentially worse, though. Not only did the sociopaths in D.C. and governments around the world derail the economy, but they made it a crime for people to socialize, as we mentioned earlier. The only thing worse than being bankrupt is being bankrupt and alone. Specifically, individuals lost their money because of politicians and were prohibited from spending time with loved ones because of politicians.

Sickeningly, leftist sociopaths seem to care more about the fact that black people[103] lost more jobs than white people than they do about the greatest reduction of human prosperity in world history.

Politicians responded to the crash they caused by spending trillions and trillions of taxpayer dollars. As we discussed earlier, this money went to their cronies, and they gave a tiny percentage of it back to taxpayers, who took the bait and gratefully accepted their own money back from the tyrants, oblivious to the fact that they were receiving pennies for each dollar that was stolen from them by politicians.

The federal government only collects around four trillion dollars[104] each year in taxes. How will politicians pay for the 6+ trillion dollars[105] that they recklessly spent on corona-fascism in addition to their regular annual expenses?

Well…it's complicated. But it likely has something to do with borrowing and printing trillions of dollars, neither of which are very good for our economy. The borrowing will plunge us further into debt (the united states government's debt just hit 28 trillion) and the reckless printing will further devalue the dollar. If you thought inflation was bad in recent years, just wait until the market prices in the new monetary infusion of trillions of new dollars. Maybe Democrats will get their wish after all: Venezuela in America.

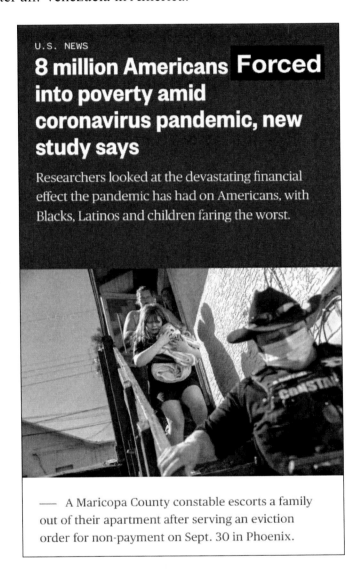

U.S. NEWS

8 million Americans Forced into poverty amid coronavirus pandemic, new study says

Researchers looked at the devastating financial effect the pandemic has had on Americans, with Blacks, Latinos and children faring the worst.

—— A Maricopa County constable escorts a family out of their apartment after serving an eviction order for non-payment on Sept. 30 in Phoenix.

Chapter 10

BRING ON THE RECESSION!

HOW DID RADICAL LEFTISTS FEEL about the recession caused by politicians shutting down businesses? They loved it. I believe there are two reasons why they were happy to see the economy destroyed and society crippled.

1) Although the united states economy is generally a "venture socialist[106]" one, our politicians claim that we are a capitalist nation, especially when it comes to naming a scapegoat for economic downturns or "income inequality." Of course, a capitalist country would be one with no regulations, taxes, or government-sanctioned violations of property rights. The great "America" has plenty of the above, meaning that it is far from a purely capitalist nation. Whenever politicians see a recession,[107] they are quick to blame capitalism[108] and use that as justification for even more socialism (government control over the economy).

2) While President Trump was in office, the evil leftists made it very clear they would do anything to make him fail, even if it hurt the country. They wanted to show everyone that Trump and his (slightly less socialist) policies were horrible and that he was evil and incompetent.

As President Trump continued to cut regulations, support an "America first" agenda, and lower taxes, the progressive left went into panic mode. The united states economy was white-hot, and employment, wages, and production were at the best levels they've been in modern times. Once the coronavirus began to spread, the Democrats seized the opportunity to finally throw a wrench into the roaring economy that was unleashed by Trump's incredible decision to get out of the way and let the market do what it does best.

Let me be clear. I am not claiming that the coronavirus was 100% cooked up by American Democrats to derail the economy and hurt Trump. I believe that the virus exists and that Democrats are evil and opportunistic power-hungry sociopaths who capitalized on a terrible situation to hurt Trump and other American workers.

Democratic TV personality Bill Maher[109] boldly admitted[110] this on his HBO show:

> *"By the way, I'm hoping for it because one way you get rid of Trump is a crashing economy. So please, bring on the recession!"*

Knowing what you now know about economic recessions being directly related to increased deaths from suicide, poor health, drugs, abuse, and more, you can begin to see how sadistic that statement was. Of course, Democratic politicians likely felt the same way, whether they said so as publicly and plainly as Maher or not.

Needless to say, the Democrats all followed the plan perfectly. They blamed Trump for the virus and for every policy he enacted in response to the virus. Predictably, the narrative quickly became "Trump did nothing to stop COVID and he is responsible for killing millions of Americans and for killing our economy!"

And a critical mass of Americans fell for it.

Chapter 11

AN UNPRECEDENTED ELECTION

BEGINNING TO WORK ON THE plan to use COVID to defeat Trump at the beginning of 2020 gave Democrats nearly a year to accomplish their goal.

Knowing very well how easy it is to "increase voter turnout" when widespread mail-in voting is permitted, Democrats had their work cut out for them. They would push corona-paranoia nonstop with every resource they had in order to convince everyone to stay home out of fear for their lives.

I remember thinking how strange it was that corona-porn (fear-porn based on the coronavirus being the most dangerous thing in history) consumed nearly 100% of the time on every TV channel, from CNN to Fox. I knew that, in today's insanely fast-paced world of news and politics, each story usually lasts only a matter of seconds or minutes. Turn on the TV an hour later, and even the political opinion shows would be talking about entirely new stories. But starting in early 2020 and lasting until election day, it seemed like the only thing that anyone on TV could talk about was corona-paranoia and how Trump botched the COVID response. This was totally calculated. The paranoia would make people stay home, kill the economy, and cause people to support "emergency" mail-in voting laws. The constant blaming of Trump for everything would do the usual job of convincing the undecided voters to oppose Trump and support Biden.

It wasn't just TV stations. YouTube, Google, Facebook, Twitter, and every other media company seemed to completely embrace the corona-paranoia.

Major stores like Walmart, Starbucks, and Home Depot fell in line with the leftist agenda to spread fear and remove Trump, and began supporting unprecedented levels of paranoia and restrictions on customers. As we mentioned in the discussion on cronyism, the wealthiest individuals and companies in the united states are nearly all in bed with politicians. They are primarily allied with Democrats, but they donate to all politicians because they enjoy special treatment from lawmakers, regardless of which party is in power. Who was not part of that group of career politicians? Donald Trump. Worse yet, Trump decreased regulations, which made it easier for smaller businesses to compete with the big players like Walmart. This did not go over very well for the billionaire class.

As corona-paranoia gained momentum, the media, big business, and anti-Trump and anti-freedom activists throughout the united states all began to pressure state and local politicians to "do something."

States like California, New York, and New Jersey quickly shut down businesses, churches (more on that later), and schools. While leftists love having the power to indoctrinate children during nearly all of their waking hours, they understood that they needed to shake the world of every parent in the united states. What better way to flip a parent's world upside down than by closing their child's school indefinitely? Being forced to stay at home to watch their children caused the Americans who didn't lose their jobs yet to take sick days or quit their jobs altogether. This caused desperation for parents, who were suddenly determined to do anything to be able to get their kids back to school so they could get back to work.

Of course, schools didn't really stop indoctrinating, controlling, and abusing children. They actually increased their control over children in some ways. As nearly every school in the united states went virtual, teachers got the chance to see children in their homes via video chat.

Any child who lived in a conservative home was suddenly at risk of being exposed and ostracized. One child had a toy gun in his house. Other children had conservative parents who said things that did not align with radical leftism. Teachers could hear background chatter around the house and see non-leftist items in the house. Talk about losing privacy!

Authoritarian socialists are often brilliant opportunists. They can easily turn any negative or neutral event into a positive toward their goal, which is to increase their power over individuals by eliminating our privacy and freedom.

Being that politicians are risk-averse by nature, and considering how much they desire to be liked by people and the media, this plan worked like a charm. While smaller states and tiny towns are often more conservative and libertarian, the small population also allows a tiny group of leftist activists or other small pressure campaigns to easily sway a local politician.

All of a sudden, politicians in states from Wyoming to Georgia began to fully endorse corona-fascism. They simply could not withstand the pressure from every influential institution in the united states.

Even Trump himself caved to the pressure and appointed swamp doctors like Birx and Fauci to lead the coronavirus response for the federal government. Trump largely agreed with the mainstream narrative about COVID, and he was hopelessly behind in the election before he even knew what hit him.

Constantly bombarding Americans with corona-mania from every single angle worked better than anyone could have imagined.

By the time November came around, the narrative throughout "America" was settled:

> *Trump is an incompetent racist who mishandled the COVID response at every turn, and we must all vote for Biden — but we must vote by mail, because we will surely die if we go outside.*

Still, at least 73 million Americans voted for Donald Trump in November. But the damage had been done, and Biden's lead was insurmountable. The record 65 million Americans[111] who voted by mail easily put Biden over the top.

I could write an entire book about the integrity of the 2020 election, but it would prevent this book from being published, my life would be destroyed by the radical American left, and it is hardly the point of this book. Suffice it to say that I never trusted elections, and that the 2020 election of "bumbling Biden" was about as trustworthy as a truck stop sushi roll.

In an effort to get out in front of the widespread concerns about Biden's mental competence and the integrity of the election, the elites quickly invented the "Office of the President-Elect." Right after election day (but not after election month) while many mail-in ballots were still being counted and certified, Democrats helped Biden hobble up to a podium and deliver regular statements from the bogus (yet official-sounding) office of the soon-to-be president.

And just like that, Americans on all sides of the issue were conditioned to accept that Biden was the duly elected president. The main objective of the socialist elites was complete. Now what?

Chapter 12

A NEW RELIGION IS BORN

AS THE MAJORITY OF AMERICANS became brainwashed by peer pressure, unprecedented media campaigns, and constant bombardment from every institution in the united states, a new religion came into prominence: The Corona-Cult, also known as the "Religion of the Mask."

Within a few short weeks, regular citizens were buying into the recommendations by Birx and Fauci. Regular people became paranoid; if you got within six feet of them or allowed your mask to slip beneath your nose, they would scold you. Some would even call the police. These reckless COVID-deniers were a danger to public health, after all!

Some politicians even proposed legislation that would make it "criminal assault" to disobey an order from other civilians[112] who commanded you to put on a mask, maintain a six-foot distance, or obey any other health-related order.

Religious zealots made a public display of their fidelity to their sacred commandments:

1) *Thou shalt wear a mask at all times*

2) *Hugging and kissing are an abomination unto God*

3) *Six feet of distance shall be maintained from others at all times*

4) *All gatherings of people shall be a sin and a desecration to the Lord*

5) *Upon being exposed to a person with any symptom, thou shalt self-quarantine*

6) *Thou shalt not seek to work, for the Lord will provide for thee*

7) *All blame for worldly problems lay at the feet of Trump, for he is the devil*

8) *Lord Biden is the savior chosen by God Almighty*

9) *Thou shalt worship healthcare workers; medical experts must be obeyed*

10) *The word of the Lord shall not be questioned; heresy is condemned by God*

Even when totally alone, these devout Covidians wore a mask. They took pictures with masks and showed them off on social media. Over the span of a few months, Covidians turned masking into a powerful signal of one's virtue, putting the supposed safety benefits of masking on the back burner. Public health is important, but publicly worshipping God is even more important. Even in video meetings,[113] participants were told by politicians to wear masks.

This new religion[114] spread like wildfire, and quickly became the predominant religion in "America." The Religion of the Mask actually enjoyed widespread adoption all over the world, boasting around 7 billion new believers at its peak. Few people in the world dared speak out against the religion, for fear of being ostracized or killed.[115] As we often observe when it comes to radical leftist control-freaks, their goals often are regressive in nature. In this case, they successfully regressed the world hundreds of years, all the way back to the age[116] when questioning the church[117] could cost a heretic his or her life.

Concurrently, other religions were being crushed. More so than a lack of faith, it was politicians literally making it a crime to attend church[118] or synagogue.[119] The megalomaniacs were determined to destroy all religions except their own.

All over the united states, politicians and their enforcers were prohibiting people from worshipping their Gods by praying in churches, mosques, synagogues, and temples. Unlike some laws that are not enforced, police officers enthusiastically punished Christians and Jews[120] for the crime of praying together. Church congregations quickly adapted to the new laws, and some churches began to hold prayers in their parking lots with worshippers remaining in their own vehicles. When cops began to punish people[121] who were praying in their own vehicles, some Christians began to realize that corona-fascism was not about safety; it was about control and crushing non-approved religions.

Central to the Jewish faith is praying in large groups in a holy temple, called a synagogue. Also referred to as a "shul" by orthodox Jews, their house of worship is respected and treated as a sacred temple. While they technically could pray anywhere, observant Jews believe that it's extremely important to pray in a synagogue that includes a Torah (Bible) and at least 10 Jewish adult men. As their houses of worship were closed by the government, Jews all over the united states began to look for ways around the law. Some of them surely violated the law and prayed in their synagogues. Some obeyed the tyrants and prayed alone in their homes. Personal friends of mine turned their own homes into synagogues, and some actually obtained a Torah and everything else they needed in order to convert their basement into a proper shul. One person I know invited nine other men to pray at his home, and they were able to satisfy their religious obligations and worship their God in the way they desired.

Of course, this person (who surely considers himself a law-abiding citizen) willfully violated numerous laws, including social distancing laws, large gathering laws, zoning laws, and likely a few others.

Many religious individuals were less hardcore and more obedient, though. Millions of Americans remained at home and complied with the demands of their politicians. Some of the individuals realized that these laws violated nearly every part of the First Amendment, meaning that they should be considered unconstitutional, illegal, and void. Many others remained totally ignorant of the constitutional violations.

Regardless of how much was understood by the public, corona-fascism was just getting started.

Chapter 13

MOVING THE GOALPOSTS

A COMMON THEME THROUGHOUT THE corona-fascism pandemic was (and still is, as of this writing) the perpetual moving of the goalposts. If a football team slowly and methodically moved the ball down the field, and the goal line was moved back 60 yards as soon as they cracked the red zone, they would not be very happy. Move the goalposts back 50 times throughout the game with no real justification, and the offense would go insane. The team moving the goalposts would be thrilled, though. They would be in total control, they would be winning, and their opponents would be powerless, frustrated, and desperate.

On March 16th, 2020, the Trump Coronavirus Task Force announced[122] the "15 Days To Slow The Spread" initiative. The initiative began to condition all 330 million sheep in the united states to obey authority, especially Dr. Birx and Dr. Fauci, both of whom are D.C. elites. The "guidelines" instructed people to stay home if they felt less than perfectly healthy. The corona-fascists also advised people to quarantine themselves if they were exposed to a person with the virus or any symptoms, including a headache, fever, nausea, diarrhea, or any other symptom. Already, they were conditioning people to think of the coronavirus as "super-Ebola."

The tyrants in charge knew that this initiative was perfect, because it set the foundation for a perpetually moving target. After the 15 days, the politicians could easily extend the lockdown. They would claim they really didn't want to, but they had to extend the restrictions because people didn't comply well enough. This "compliance" game remained a common theme throughout the tyrannical reign of terror, and it still remains in use as of this writing.

Early on, Fauci and other officials told the public that they should not wear masks. A few days prior, Dr. Jerome Adams,[123] the US surgeon general (the top health official in the US. government) strongly advised the public against the regular use of masks for coronavirus protection:

> *"Seriously, people — STOP BUYING MASKS! They are NOT effective in preventing the general public from catching Coronavirus, but if healthcare providers can't get them to care for sick patients, it puts them and our communities at risk!"*

In April, Dr. Robert Redfield,[124] the director of the Centers for Disease Control, said there was no reason for healthy people to wear masks.

Dr. Fauci[125], the director of the National Institute of Allergy and Infectious Diseases, said of the coronavirus in January of 2020:

> *"This is not a major threat to the people of the United States and this is not something that the citizens of the United States should be worried about right now."*

Fauci also said that people should not wear a mask[126] unless they were confirmed to have the virus, and that masks did not really help much against respiratory viruses, anyway.

"The virus is not spreading in the general community.... We don't routinely recommend the use of face masks by the public to prevent respiratory illness. And we certainly are not recommending that at this time for this new virus," said Dr. Nancy Messonnier[127], director of the National Center for Immunization and Respiratory Diseases.

"The average healthy person does not need to have a mask, and they shouldn't be wearing masks.... I've never seen a person practice hand hygiene before removing a mask in public and then after removing the mask.... There's no evidence that wearing masks on healthy people will protect them," said Dr. Eli Perencevich[128], a professor of medicine and epidemiology at the University of Iowa's College of Medicine, according to Forbes.

Of course, these experts and all the others who said that masks either are not necessary, don't stop a virus that is infinitesimally smaller than the mask's holes, or are downright harmful were absolutely correct. However, as the politicians realized that they could use the virus to take unprecedented amounts of freedom, money, and power from individuals, they began to change their tune.

Joining forces with their powerful allies in the "private" sector, the media, and all other influential institutions, tyrants managed to convince nearly everyone in the united states to wear a mask at all times. A few people refused to wear masks, either out of defiance or because it made it harder for them to breathe or accomplish other tasks. While politicians claimed to hate seeing non-compliance, they needed at least some level of disobedience. Those darn "COVID deniers" provided the elites with two major benefits:

1)   Cracking down on non-compliant individuals sends a mes-

sage to all others who consider disobedience that they must obey. Videos of non-masked men[129] being brutally dragged off of buses[130] by police and stories about the mothers who were arrested by cops for bringing their children[131] to a park spread all over the world. Such stories[132] served as examples to anyone who considered standing up to corona-fascism.

2)   If they could demonstrate that even one person in the united states failed to comply with all of the health recommendations for even one second, the tyrants could justify extending the corona-fascism for another 90 days.

Many stories of totally healthy individuals who did not wear the magical mask being beaten or shamed for their "crimes" successfully kept the majority of citizens in nearly every state on Earth in compliance with the guidelines. Additionally, many strong pressures — all ultimately coming from politicians — caused businesses to make masks mandatory in their stores. By the summer, nearly everyone in the united states was well-trained and followed mask mandates religiously.

Little did they know that corona-fascism was just getting started.

Although it had been nearly a year since the "worst pandemic ever" came to the united states, some people were clearly still alive by the fall of 2020. In fact, nobody that I know even knows of anyone who died of coronavirus. In New Hampshire, only a few people died from COVID, and over 62% of them were older than 80 years old[133]. Only around 13% were under 70 years old. Still, our dictator, Chris Sununu, implemented some of the harshest lockdown measures in the united states.

In order for the politicians to force everyone to obey draconian restrictions and destroy their own lives, the elites needed to move another goalpost: Asymptomatic transmission. In January of 2020, Lord Fauci said that people who do not have the **virus and symptoms** have essentially zero likelihood[134] of spreading the virus to others. The few people who really do have the virus (as opposed to a false positive) without any symptoms tend to have such a low level of the viral load that they cannot infect others.

Fauci said at a press conference in January that:

> *"In all the history of respiratory-borne viruses of any type, asymptomatic transmission has never been the driver of outbreaks. The driver of outbreaks is ALWAYS a symptomatic person."*

Needless to say, the D.C. professionals were quick to flip the script and proclaim that, regardless of whether a person had any symptoms or felt healthy as a horse, all humans in the world should be presumed to be infected and super-contagious. This was even applied to the millions of people who were totally immune[135] to the virus because they had it months prior and gained immunity to coronavirus for life. Also, a study of 10 million people[136] found almost no evidence of asymptomatic spread.

In January of 2021, Dr. Fauci came up with another brilliant idea: If wearing one mask was good, wearing two masks[137] was plus-good[138]! Immediately, dictators[139] around the united states began to push double masking[140]. Remember the 10th Commandment?

Even months prior, Fauci was wise to set himself up for the potential goggle mandate. In July, Fauci recommended wearing goggles[141], explaining that we really should protect all mucus membranes in the body from the super-deadly virus:

"You have mucosa in the nose, mucosa in the mouth, but you also have mucosa in the eye...theoretically, you should protect all the mucosal surfaces. So if you have goggles or an eye shield you should use it."

Unlike the holy masks, goggles were not widely adopted by healthy individuals. Maybe people realized by July that if the virus killed nobody they knew in eight full months of "raging through the country," they would probably survive without eye protection.

The entire premise of corona-fascism was initially based on the "flatten the curve" theory. This meant the elites did not even aim to *stop* the virus or even to *decrease* the number of infections. The plan was simply to flatten the spike of new severe infections over a longer period of time so the medical system did not get overwhelmed with 100 million critically ill patients in one week. That would be disastrous. Of course, "flatten the curve" quickly morphed into "just wear the damned mask and end all social interactions until a vaccine is available."

In October of 2020, Trump signaled that the vaccine was coming along well, and that it would be available around election time. Democrats made it their top priority to ensure that a vaccine — or any other good news — could not be made public until after the election of Biden. Voters must be totally convinced that Trump is the devil and that nothing good can occur[142] in this world until Saint Biden becomes President. Remember the 8th Commandment?

The election was (mostly) over and, by December, the first COVID vaccines[143] were administered to healthcare workers, with plans to expand availability to millions of other high-priority individuals within the next few weeks. With Pfizer-BioNTech's vaccine showing 95% efficacy[144] in trials, and with Moderna and J&J producing their own nearly perfect vaccines, Americans finally had some hope, right?

How naive they were!

The elites initially said that once 90% of Americans were vaccinated[145], we could return to normal. Maybe we could finally ditch the masks, go to work, and see our loved ones again. Biden even said that by July 4th[146], we might be allowed to spend a bit of time with family to celebrate our independence from tyranny, as long as we followed all of the government's corona-fascist guidelines, of course.

With 29 million people having natural immunity to COVID (from previous infection) and another 75 million[147] being vaccinated by the middle of March, one might think that we could start discussing a return to normalcy.

On the other hand, Fauci did say that corona-fascism could continue until 2022[148]. The World Health Organization has said that it could be five more years[149] until we could return to normal. As the vaccine began to reach more Americans at the start of 2021, the control-freaks knew they needed to move the goalposts once more. Reports of multiple "variants" of the virus were like music to the ears of politicians and other sociopaths. By March of 2021, the tyrants and their cronies had a perfect narrative[150] in place: Coronavirus variants from Britain[151] are exponentially more contagious and much more deadly, and will infect everyone in the world and kill us all if we don't embrace even more corona-fascism. Furthermore, they warned, natural immunity and the vaccines will be ineffective against the new strains of COVID so we may need to wait even longer before we can have our lives back.

The story of the British variants was followed by reports of South African[152] strains, and then of Brazilian[153] strains, all of which were so contagious and deadly that they could kill all life in the universe in an instant. Worse yet, there were now thousands of different strains[154] of coronavirus all over the world. Hope began to fade once more.

While the initial plan may have been to return to normal once Trump was gone so they could hail Biden as the savior of humanity for ending COVID, I believe that the elites called an audible sometime around the election. They likely realized that they could transition the Trump narrative out of the media cycle, and guide the narrative in the direction of the "new normal," which would involve permanent sacrifices[155] of individual liberty and privacy. Trump was already gone and the Democrats totally controlled every part of the government. They hardly needed Trump as a scapegoat anymore. Of course, they would still mention Trump whenever they needed to blame someone for anything that went wrong, but they no longer had to wind down the corona-fascism. The party could continue!

On March 17th, Senator Rand Paul confronted[156] Fauci about the constant moving of the goalposts in a Senate hearing. Dr. Paul mentioned many studies proving that people with natural or acquired immunity to viruses could remain immune for decades, not months, like Fauci implied. Fauci defended his recommendation to continue wearing masks indefinitely, regardless of whether a person had the virus and the vaccine. Paul continually asked Fauci if there was any evidence of a person getting sick after being vaccinated, and Fauci could not point to any.

What's next for corona-fascism's ever-moving goalposts?

The possibilities are endless!

The elites might demand that everyone engage in contact tracing, which people are largely already doing. They could place an RFID tracker on (or in) our bodies so they could track our movements[157] and alert people when they are exposed to coronavirus. They could use this same program for the next pandemic or every flu season!

Politicians might mandate flu-fascism every winter. After all, the seasonal flu is similar to COVID in terms of contagiousness and lethality.

They might make people wear masks whenever they want to gather in groups beyond a certain density.

The bottom line is that elite politicians and their evil cronies will continue to move the goalposts as long as they can get away with doing so. We can all agree that we will never again get back to the normal social life we once enjoyed. No, things will never be normal again. It's right there in one of the corona-fascist's favorite slogans: "The New Normal."

Chapter 14

HYPOCRISY

WHILE THE TYRANTS AND THEIR obedient sheep were perpetuating the paranoia and preaching the gospel of corona-fascism, many elites and progressives neglected to obey the sacred commandments of their own religion.

The two doctors who directed the federal government's response to the virus were Dr. Deborah Birx and Doctor Anthony Fauci. In addition to being well-established residents of the swamp, both doctors are world-class hypocrites. Despite preaching the gospel of the mask, Fauci ditched his mask once it became uncomfortable while sitting right next to other people at a Nationals baseball game.

It should be pointed out that Fauci was with his wife and a friend, with nobody else anywhere near their section. Still, all three of them did start the game with their masks on, clearly indicating that masks were still warranted. If masks were not necessary when spending time with relatives, the three elites would not have worn them at all. When the photo of Fauci clearly enjoying the game for a prolonged period without a mask (while his friend kept his mask on), Fauci lied to a reporter[158] and claimed that he only lowered his mask briefly to take a sip of water because he was super-dehydrated. Fauci used a few other excuses: The person he was talking and laughing with was a super close friend, and Lord Fauci also told the reporter that he tested negative just one day prior to the game.

All of these excuses are considered totally unacceptable when we peasants are punished for failing to wear a mask, but elite politicians like Fauci can use any excuses they desire. In the same segment, Fauci criticizes anyone who talks about his hypocrisy as "mischievous."

Fauci's partner in corona-fascism, Dr. Birx, also violated her own rules. After demanding that nobody travel to another household for Thanksgiving, White House COVID coordinator Deborah Birx did just that[159]. She figured that, as an elite Lord, the rules didn't apply to her.

We know that politicians are above the law, but the hypocrisy in this instance is more meaningful than just plain corruption. If Fauci and Birx thought the virus was as dangerous as they claimed it was, they would follow all of their recommendations to a tee — because they would not want to die. By violating their own safety guidelines, they are undermining their own credibility when it comes to public health policy.

Politicians like Dictator Newsom[160] enjoyed trips to Maui while locking his peasants down in California. My own dictator, Chris Sununu, only seems to wear a mask for photo-ops.

Pro-freedom foundation Heritage.org[161] is trying to track all of the politicians who have violated their own corona-fascism rules with an online map tool. I do not envy whoever was tasked with that impossible job. The map only shows 62 incidents of politicians violating COVID guidelines, but I am sure that there are thousands of other cases of hypocrisy.

Of course, illegal aliens who cross the border[162] are barely restricted by COVID. Biden has been allowing them to flow into the[163] united states. without any sort of vetting process since he took office. Surely, immigrants could not possibly have coronavirus, right?

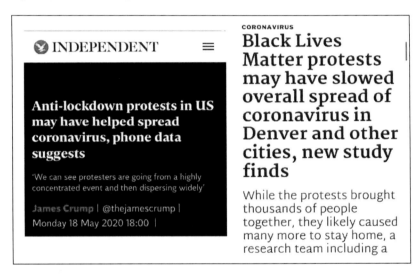

Throughout the entire "pandemic," anti-freedom, anti-Trump groups were not only allowed to gather in huge crowds with no social distancing, but they were encouraged to do so by politicians. Indeed, praying in a church with masks and social distancing is unacceptable and illegal, but thousands of rioters in tightly packed groups were allowed to protest as much as they wanted. Of course, the leftist media[164] covered for BLM and encouraged[165] the riots while denying that such gatherings could possibly spread[166] COVID. In fact, leftist dictators and mayors stood inches from the other protestors as they marched with BLM[167] to demand more communism and worse treatment of whites.

Pro-freedom protests were not acceptable. Anti-conservative BLM protests were totally amazing.

Laws only restrict peasants like you and me. The Lords are exempt from their own laws.

Simple enough, right?

Chapter 15

THE OBSOLETE LEGISLATURE

ONE OF THE PHENOMENA THAT occurred during the pandemic involved the separation of powers. Under normal circumstances, the government of each state, and the federal government had a few branches, each of which had specific authority. Each branch was designed to hold the others in check to some extent. Corona-fascism destroyed that model.

In New Hampshire and in all 50 states, the government is generally divided into the executive branch, the legislative branch, and the judicial branch. The founders granted the power to write and vote on legislation (laws) exclusively to the legislature. In most states, the legislature is composed of a House and a Senate. Governors were granted the power to sign or veto legislation and to execute the laws passed by the aforementioned process. The judges within the judicial branch were granted the authority to rule on ambiguous cases by utilizing the law as their guide.

Once the federal government declared a national emergency, nearly every governor in the united states used that opportunity to declare states of emergency. This allowed tyrannical governors to usurp legislative authority from the legislators and begin to write, pass, and enforce laws on their own, without any oversight or accountability. During the entire 2020, the legislative process ground to a halt, and legislators became totally impotent; they could no longer do the two things they were elected to do: propose and vote on legislation.

To the best of my knowledge, the various COVID restrictions in every state came about via illegal executive orders by the governors; not a single state legislature passed a single bill. And such is the story of how just about every governor became a dictator.

Anyone who knows basic civics understands that executives (governors, presidents, etc.) have certain powers they can exercise in true emergencies in which waiting for the legislature to meet and pass a bill would lead to catastrophe (such as a missile from a foreign enemy being in the air and orders to stop the missile must be made within a few seconds). Of course, the coronavirus was hardly an emergency of that magnitude to begin with. It was not a missile or bomb that was going to land in a matter of seconds, and it was not going to be over in a few minutes. The virus is here to stay for a few months – or years!

Even if we assume that the initial lockdowns and mask mandates last winter were emergent and could not have waited for legislatures to convene, there is simply no justification for continuing to rule over the people by executive order a year later. This is especially true in an age when legislators could easily meet and conduct their business by phone, internet, email, or video conference. They can meet in large enough venues to remain socially distant from one another. In fact, the New Hampshire House of Representatives — the largest state legislative chamber in the united states — has had sessions in such venues. Yet, this chamber and all other chambers have neglected to pass any bills regarding COVID restrictions for the past 12 months. Further, they have weakly turned a blind eye and allowed their governors to act like dictators and rule over the people the legislators themselves were elected to represent. As far as this author is concerned, every legislature in the united states has rendered itself impotent. Maybe we should consider eliminating legislatures entirely.

Are Republicans any better?

Not really. Other than Kristi Noem of South Dakota, every American governor has violated their citizens. This includes the 22 states in which executive orders were enacted by Republican dictators, with no real opposition from Republican legislatures[168].

State legislators are obsolete, and there is no place for them in the post-corona world in which we are ruled by a few dictators.

Chapter 16

STILL SUPPORT CORONA-FASCISM?

WHAT WOULD I SAY TO those readers who are still totally okay with severe restrictions in the name of COVID?

If you believe that politicians should have the rightful authority to do whatever it takes to ensure public health, I harbor no hate toward you!

I just have one favor to ask of you.

When the minority of people who reject corona-fascism (or tyranny in general) inevitably form their own society, let them go. Don't tell your politicians to send men with guns to murder those who don't agree with your policies. Many individuals on both sides of the aisle have stated they would support using the military to stop a state or a geographical area from governing itself.

This group of people will live far enough from you that they would not pose any risk of infecting you with COVID or anything else. They will have their own economy, education systems, medical systems, and all other institutions. You won't have to worry about these reckless jerks harming you or your society in any way.

Before COVID, many people were blissfully ignorant of the division[169] within the united states. But now that corona-fascism has exposed that there are at least two different cultures trying to live together in this country, I'd like to think that nearly everyone understands that a divorce is inevitable. Not every person in "America" can peacefully coexist. And that is perfectly okay. We clearly do not all have the same set of values. And that is okay.

Many people in the united states value public health above all. These people are okay with politicians restricting freedom and diminishing privacy for the sake of public health. Dictator Sununu made it very clear that he identified with this group when he said:

"Public health first. Always.[170]"

Many people in the united states prioritize equality of outcomes[171] above all. These people are okay with politicians manipulating the economy in a way that redistributes money from people who have a lot to those who have very little.

A minority of people believe in personal liberty above all. Some individuals, including this author, believe that personal freedom is the most important thing and that no politician or cop should ever violate personal freedom, no matter the justification.

As you surely realize, the various groups cannot live together in one nation under one set of laws because that set of laws would always be incompatible with at least a large portion of the population.

So, what is the solution?

Personally, I believe that if each state could generally govern itself (as the founders intended), we would be 90% of the way to my ideal arrangement for society.

Ultimately, I believe that the more local the policymakers, and the more accountable the government, the better.

So if this book made you angry or offended you, and if you believe that I am a psychopath, dangerous, or that my values are incompatible with yours, let that serve as the ultimate evidence that we cannot live together. You and I have completely different sets of values. And, without common values, people cannot coexist in one society.

I'm sorry, but I think we need to break up.

THANK YOU

Thank you so much for reading my book about corona-fascism. I know that you could have spent your time, money, and energy reading any other book in the world, and I sincerely appreciate that you chose mine. If you found that this book provided any value to you, please leave a review on Amazon. It could be done in under a minute, and it would REALLY help the book gain exposure to more readers like you. If you think that a particular friend would enjoy — or be offended — by reading this book, please share it with them, too!

Thank you so much!

-Alu

ADDITIONAL EVIDENCE OF CORRUPTION, INFLATED STATISTICS, AND CORONA-FASCISM

1. Peer-reviewed study: Ivermectin cuts COVID infections, deaths by 75%: https://www.wnd.com/2021/02/peer-reviewed-study-ivermectin-cuts-covid-infections-deaths-75/

2. Lancet No Effect On Mortality Paper: https://thefatemperor.com/wp-content/uploads/2020/11/1.-LANCET-LOCKDOWN-NO-MORTALITY-BENEFIT-A-country-level-analysis-measuring-the-impact-of-government-actions.pdf

3. Was Lockdown in Germany Necessary? – Homburg: https://thefatemperor.com/wp-content/uploads/2020/11/2.-Was-Lockdown-in-Germany-Necessary-Homburg.pdf

4. Koch Institute Germany Analysis: https://thefatemperor.com/wp-content/uploads/2020/11/3.-KOCH-INSTITUTE-Epi-Report-R0-down-to-1-before-lockdown.pdf

5. Bristol University Paper: https://thefatemperor.com/wp-content/uploads/2020/11/4.-PREPRINT-BRISTOL-Did-COVID-19-infections-decline-before-UK-lockdown.pdf

6. Nature Submission Flaxman et al Response: https://thefatemperor.com/wp-content/uploads/2020/11/5.-PREPRINT-LOCKDOWN-HOMBURG-2020-Comment-Flaxman-SAGE-Neil-Ferguson-Sham-Paper-on-Lives-Saved.pdf

7. Professor Ben Israel Analysis: https://thefatemperor.com/wp-content/uploads/2020/11/6.-PREPRINT-LOCKDOWN-ADDED-LITTLE-OR-NOTHING-PROF-BEN-ISRAEL.pdf

8. NIH Paper: https://thefatemperor.com/wp-content/uploads/2020/11/7.-PREPRINT-LOCKDOWN-NIH-Impact-of-non-pharmaceutical-interventions-against-COVID-19-in-Europe.pdf

9. Woods Hole Institute Paper: https://thefatemperor.com/wp-content/uploads/2020/11/8.-PREPRINT-WOODS-HOLE-Full-lockdown-policies-in-Western-Europe-countries-have-no-evident.pdf

10. Edinburgh Stratclyde University Paper: https://thefatemperor.com/wp-content/uploads/2020/11/9.-PREPRINT-EDINBURGH-UNIVERSITY-Trajectory-of-COVID-19-epidemic-in-Europe.pdf

11. British Medical Journal BMJ Paper: https://thefatemperor.com/wp-content/uploads/2020/11/10.-BMJ-Effect-of-school-closures-on-mortality-from-coronavirus-disease-2019-old-and-new-predictions.pdf

12. Israel Massive Cost Of Lockdown Paper: https://thefatemperor.com/wp-content/uploads/2020/11/10.-PREPRINT-MILLION-DOLLAR-modeling-social-distancing-strategies-to-prevent-SARS-CoV2-spread-in-Israel-A-Cost-effectiveness-analysis.pdf

13. Epidemiology Too Little of a Good Thing Paper: https://thefatemperor.com/wp-content/uploads/2020/11/11.-EPIDEMIOLOGY-Too-Little-of-a-Good-Thing-A-Paradox-of-Moderate-Infection-Control.pdf

14. Smart Thinking: Lockdown and Covid-19 Implications for Public Policy: https://thefatemperor.com/wp-content/uploads/2020/12/13.-Smart-thinking-lockdown-and-Covid-19-Implications-for-Public-Policy.pdf

15. Scotland Life Expectancy Paper: https://thefatemperor.com/wp-content/uploads/2020/11/13.-Scotland-Actual-Impact-exceeds-Life-Expectancy-Age.pdf

16. Lockdown Costs More Lives Paper Federico: https://thefatemperor.com/wp-content/uploads/2020/11/14.-FEDERICO-SARS-CoV-2-waves-in-Europe-A-2-stratum-SEIRS-model-solution.pdf

17. Did Lockdown Work? Paper: https://thefatemperor.com/wp-content/uploads/2020/11/15.-Did-Lockdown-Work-An-Economists-Cross-Country-Comparison.pdf

18. Four Stylized Facts About COVID-19: https://thefatemperor.com/wp-content/uploads/2020/11/16.-FOUR-STYLIZED-FACTS-ABOUT-COVID-19.pdf

19. How Does Belarus...: https://thefatemperor.com/wp-content/uploads/2020/11/17.-BMJ-Covid-19-How-does-Belarus-have-one-of-the-lowest-death-rates-in-Europe.pdf

20. Living With Children In UK: https://thefatemperor.com/wp-content/uploads/2020/11/18.-Association-between-living-with-children-and-outcomes-from-COVID-19-12-million-adults-in-England.pdf

21. Pandata Country Analysis: https://thefatemperor.com/wp-content/uploads/2020/11/19.-PANDA-Exploring-inter-country-coronavirus-mortality.pdf

22. NEJM Marine Study Quarantine: https://thefatemperor.com/wp-content/uploads/2020/11/20.-NEJM-SARS-CoV-2-Transmission-among-Marine-Recruits-during-Quarantine-.pdf

23. A Matter Of Vulnerability Study: https://thefatemperor.com/wp-content/uploads/2020/11/21-Covid-19-Mortality-A-Matter-of-Vulnerability-Among-Nations-Facing-Limited-Margins-of-Adaptation.pdf

24. Global Perspective: Children at Risk: https://collateralglobal.org

25. Million Dollar Social Distancing: https://thefatemperor.com/wp-content/uploads/2020/11/1.-PREPRINT-MILLION-DOLLAR-modeling-social-distancing-strategies-to-prevent-SARS-CoV2-spread-in-Israel-A-Cost-effectiveness-analysis.pdf

26. Cost Benefit Analysis Of Lockdown: https://thefatemperor.com/wp-content/uploads/2020/11/2.-EUROPE-UK-A-cost-benefit-analysis-of-the-lockdown-in-the-United-Kingdom.pdf

27. BMJ Ioannidis Debate: https://thefatemperor.com/wp-content/uploads/2020/11/3.-BMJ-Head-to-Head-Ioannidis-Should-governments-continue-lockdown-to-slow-the-Spread.pdf

28. NIH Negative Impacts Of Lockdown: https://thefatemperor.com/wp-content/uploads/2020/11/4.-NIH-Negative-impacts-of-COVID-19-lockdown-on-mental-health-service-access-and-follow-up-adherence.pdf

29. BMJ: Herd Immunity Policy Could Save Lives: https://thefatemperor.com/wp-content/uploads/2020/11/5.-BMJ-Her-Immunity-Policy-could-have-Saved-More-Lives.pdf

30. Impact Of Lockdown Disorders: https://thefatemperor.com/wp-content/uploads/2020/11/6.-Exploring-the-impact-of-the-COVID-19-pandemic-and-UK-lockdown-on-individuals-with-experience-of-eating-disorders.pdf

31. BMJ Delayed Access To Care: https://thefatemperor.com/wp-content/uploads/2020/11/7.-BMJ-Delayed-access-to-care-and-late-presentations-in-children-during-the-COVID-19-pandemic.pdf

32. Cambridge: Living With COVID – Balancing: https://thefatemperor.com/wp-content/uploads/2020/11/8.-CAMBRIDGE-living_with_covid19_balancing_costs_against_benefits_in_the_face_of_the_virus.pdf

33. Psychiatry Research – Living With Covid: https://thefatemperor.com/wp-content/uploads/2020/11/9.-PSYCHIATRY-RESEARCH-Impact-of-COVID-19-and-lockdown-on-mental-health-of-children-and-adolescents.pdf

34. JAMA Hospitalizations For Chronic Disease: https://thefatemperor.com/wp-content/uploads/2020/11/10.-JAMA-Hospitalizations-for-Chronic-Disease-and-Acute-Conditions-in-the-Time-of-COVID-19.pdf

35. Irish Cancer Society Submission: https://thefatemperor.com/wp-content/uploads/2020/11/2020-09-30_submission-averil-power-chief-executive-irish-cancer-society-scc19r-r-0419_en.pdf

36. Eclinical Deaths of Despair: https://thefatemperor.com/wp-content/uploads/2020/11/ECLINICAL-USA-Race-COVID-19-and-deaths-of-despair.pdf

37. ONS Excess Death Mess: https://thefatemperor.com/wp-content/uploads/2020/11/ONS-April-2020_Initial_estimates_of_Excess_Deaths_from_COVID-19.pdf

38. Death by Lockdown: https://thefatemperor.com/wp-content/uploads/2020/11/PDF-Death-by-Lockdown-includes-links.pdf

39. Lockdown – A Focus On The Poor and Children: https://thefatemperor.com/wp-content/uploads/2020/11/PDF-LockDown-Study-Report-with-focus-on-Poor-and-Children.pdf

40. Mental Health and Lockdown: https://thefatemperor.com/wp-content/uploads/2020/11/PDF-UK-Site-Reachwell.org-Mental-Health-Evidence-Based.com_.pdf

41. Projected Deaths of Despair from Lockdown: https://thefatemperor.com/wp-content/uploads/2020/11/PDF-WBT_Projected-Deaths-of-Despair-150000-COVID-19.pdf

42. The Price of Panic Website: https://thefatemperor.com/wp-content/uploads/2020/11/The-Price-of-Panic-Website.pdf

43. Minnesota lawmakers say coronavirus deaths could be inflated by 40% after reviewing death certificates: https://www.washingtonexaminer.com/news/coronavirus-death-certificates-minnesota-inflated

44. Conservative Review with Daniel Horowitz - Ep 734 | We Need a Debate Over the Facts on the Virus on Stitcher:

https://www.stitcher.com/podcast/conservative-review/
the-conservative-conscience-with-daniel-horowitz/e/78423666

45. Long-term Mask Use May Contribute to Advanced Stage Lung Cancer, Study Finds: https://www.globalresearch.ca/long-term-mask-use-may-contribute-advanced-stage-lung-cancer-study-finds/5736339

46. House report says Florida's COVID-19 death toll inflated by 10%: https://www.thecentersquare.com/florida/house-report-says-floridas-covid-19-death-toll-inflated-by-10/article_5af31f72-0e6b-11eb-bd2a-a38383a03f07.html

47. CDC admits that only 9,000 people (6% of the amount previously thought) have died from COVID alone; the others had multiple other illnesses: https://www.cdc.gov/nchs/nvss/vsrr/covid_weekly/index.htm?fbclid=IwAR3xKJr99G0g1GR0JnwjDJPkL31ULal_7jucec8Cncec4k79v63DL8kCBGE#Comorbidities

48. The Sneaky Trick a Public Health Official Used to Make Mask Mandates Look Super Effective: https://fee.org/articles/the-sneaky-trick-a-public-health-official-used-to-make-mask-mandates-look-super-effective/?utm_source=email&utm_medium=email&utm_campaign=2020_FEEDaily&fbclid=IwAR27rwpZHP3yyjRUqW4Zg_xAIfWStTa44CfREyVNa7-syKHDA1-mGgTmIro

49. 'We see no point in wearing a face mask,' Sweden's top virus expert says as he touts the country's improving COVID numbers: https://fortune.com/2020/07/29/no-point-in-wearing-mask-sweden-covid/?fbclid=IwAR1COard8BWmOV9z-V18_1im9a0hEp5KLtzC0D3zn-P2OfgJ4K0ab52OX9Bo

50. 600,000 people were told they had COVID-19 despite not being tested: https://thepostmillennial.com/600-000-people-were-told-they-had-covid-19-despite-not-being-tested?fbclid=IwAR14PqHNAWtRTf5Iuxm4RAzpAMLLPfdbg36xlyovB-DyVEG3eVqSNGmeY20

51. CDC Head Estimates U.S. Coronavirus Cases Might be 10 Times Higher Than Data Show: https://time.com/5859790/cdc-coronavirus-estimates/?utm_source=facebook&utm_medium=social&utm_campaign=editorial&utm_term=health_covid-19&linkId=91880756&fbclid=IwAR1MlGUeXAwbDT9-DPo3_oH6-CGctP6izkJDJZ30U28jShhKq6jxIheqP24

52. Yale Professor of epidemiology says Hydroxychloroquine cures COVID (leftists continue to imply that the drug is the most dangerous substance on Earth and does not help in the treatment of COVID at all):

https://www.newsweek.com/key-defeating-covid-19-already-exists-we-need-start-using-it-opinion-1519535?fbclid=IwAR2KX94UO7ghoVgn5i6K-n0Z0y4uipFnrFQsLmoQwK_v6pSpRiYY8J0oZLc

53. Georgia kicks off chilling door-to-door COVID-19 blood collections: https://www.washingtontimes.com/news/c020/apr/28/georgia-kicks-chilling-door-door-covid-19-blood-co/?fbclid=IwAR2OpqPOxLUkYhe5U4JpnsdvwEiN-6pK2VFvCBl7OIBeFY8bm72RCgeF3JQ

54. Health company apologizes for falsely telling 600,000 US military members they were infected with coronavirus: https://www.theblaze.com/news/coronavirus-false-military-positives-email?fbclid=IwAR2J2iWFeNRZYKJSveAOfJpOp6TLqH0a4_vZQwhvvgucctHTtF_jIxT7zDc

55. Orange County inflated its coronavirus test numbers by mistakenly including antibody tests: https://www.msn.com/en-us/news/us/orange-county-inflated-its-coronavirus-test-numbers-by-mistakenly-including-antibody-tests-officials-say/ar-BB16hl1P?fbclid=IwAR25qNDpytLBkpp6NQ-08k99jWV6s856k38h49c0ni7o7KPGPccZJk5Iu1E

56. CDC Says Possibly 'Less Than Half' Of Positive Antibody Tests Are Correct: https://www.forbes.com/sites/tommybeer/2020/05/26/cdc-says-possibly-less-than-half-of-positive-antibody-tests-are-correct/?fbclid=IwAR10haaTRojFQBbcPMr8IIG5D2OxS_wA4s3hNidTZHC7EswUN-_41uhhBp0#442187bd2391

57. CDC adds runny nose, nausea to the growing list of COVID-19 symptoms: https://www.usatoday.com/story/news/nation/2020/07/10/coronavirus-symptoms-diarrhea-nausea-congestion-runny-nose/5412946002/?fbclid=IwAR2r_P5ghbV3HOXemtoO2zmRTwjy-QXzAADt8VRfYA3OinOWhoOUHfQPF7tc

58. 99% of Those Who Died From COVID Had Other Illness: https://www.bloomberg.com/news/articles/2020-03-18/99-of-those-who-died-from-virus-had-other-illness-italy-says?fbclid=IwAR1ekZKzUaHogsj-PCpynJcl9FhE-3LOCKCkadcqSLM2P8f4DxCnjqJcGfE

59. COVID-19 Disqualifies Citizens From Joining the Military For Life: https://www.militarytimes.com/news/your-military/2020/05/06/coronavirus-survivors-banned-from-joining-the-military/?fbclid=IwAR3omSrSbSeeM0k_VGpX0n5u8yNLr8DwURhwxxphlyJ6BFR0tR1Ntl1tAyk

60. Hospitals Get Paid More to List Patients as COVID-19 and Three Times as Much if the Patient Goes on Ventilator: https://thespectator.info/2020/04/09/hospitals-get-paid-more-to-list-patients-as-covid-19-and-three-times-as-much-if-the-patient-goes-on-ventilator-video/

61. $14M in relief funds find members of Congress and family: https://www.rollcall.com/2020/07/08/14m-in-relief-funds-find-members-and-family/?fbclid=IwAR3kchbHtY0S6
7Ie4_e6zUQbUSHPCL4gLHh0BWfUHTeYaY-nXthsVNE5xTw

62. Governors' Companies Among Recipients of Virus Relief Loans: https://www.wfmj.com/story/42330504/governors-companies-among-recipients-of-virus-relief-loans?fbclid=IwAR1AkepcomZqF5oFyET5KqxvqUlaK
97VxcXeqHVBbZXIugTOAp1QIU3zSuk

63. Tens of thousands of coronavirus tests have been double-counted, officials admit: https://www.telegraph.co.uk/global-health/science-and-disease/tens-thousands-coronavirus-tests-have-double-counted-officials/?fbclid=IwAR3LotZMu0tGBDRVdi6RA
tYR3_zddi8I9dbQC7RgBSTNZ49y3d9NH8l03rl

64. Former Health Ministry Chief Yoram Lass Calls Out 'Coronavirus Lie': https://www.jewishpress.com/news/health-and-medicine/coronavirus/former-health-ministry-chief-yoram-lass-calls-out-coronavirus-lie/2020
/07/12/?fbclid=IwAR3jMtjrxGfAKHQpUPmqAUJBQdEGtcrNszv1V4Nfnb
klK-7jIECqTCOzG0A

65. Our Endless State of Emergency and De-Facto Dictatorship: https://mises.org/power-market/our-endless-state-emergency-and-de-facto-dictatorship?fbclid=IwAR2WKdFpmdRs
NXf-oSOOrpAuwqpVFUB8l6sJhZp39NMUidAMhJ7WGXimjjA

66. The US is Dramatically Overcounting Coronavirus Deaths: https://townhall.com/columnists/johnrlottjr/2020/05/16/the-us-is-dramatically-overcounting-coronavirus-deaths-n2568925

67. Antibody tests for Covid-19 wrong up to half the time, CDC says: https://www.cnn.com/2020/05/26/health/antibody-tests-cdc-coronavirus-wrong/index.html

68. COVID-19 Herd Immunity Is Much Closer Than Antibody Tests Suggest, Say 2 New Studies: https://www.cnn.com/2020/05/26/health/antibody-tests-cdc-coronavirus-wrong/index.html

69. Fishermen test positive despite spending 35 days at sea and testing negative before they left: https://www.cnn.com/2020/05/26/health/antibody-tests-cdc-coronavirus-wrong/index.html

70. Scientists Warn CDC Testing Data Could Create Misleading Picture Of Pandemic: https://www.npr.org/sections/coronavirus-live-updates/2020/05/21/860480756/scientists-warn-cdc-testing-data-

could-create-misleading-picture-of-pandemic?fbclid=IwAR1u-G2eRb-
09DZaTzp4RIFt_YLp7gCB9RalDcrLSdtAba5Yn--nk4TmJBEE

71. Joliet Chamber Of Commerce Dived Deep Into COVID Numbers
In Will County And Found Double Counting: https://www.npr.
org/sections/coronavirus-live-updates/2020/05/21/860480756/
scientists-warn-cdc-testing-data-could-create-misleading-picture-of-
pandemic?fbclid=IwAR1u-G2eRb09DZaTzp4RIFt_YLp7gCB9RalDcrLSd-
tAba5Yn--nk4TmJBEE

72. Covid 19 — What the Data Tells Us: https://medium.com/analyticaper/
covid-19-what-the-data-tells-us-3a08e42ee36f

73. As sports resume, some fans will be made of card-
board: https://medium.com/analyticaper/
covid-19-what-the-data-tells-us-3a08e42ee36f

74. Dr. Anthony Fauci says new virus in China has traits of 2009 swine
flu and 1918 pandemic flu: https://medium.com/analyticaper/
covid-19-what-the-data-tells-us-3a08e42ee36f

75. A fiasco in the making? As the coronavirus pandemic takes hold, we
are making decisions without reliable data: https://www.statnews.
com/2020/03/17/a-fiasco-in-the-making-as-the-coronavirus-
pandemic-takes-hold-we-are-making-decisions-without-reliable-
data/?fbclid=IwAR2wcWfXTMtVgPyxINZNstbk5uPM8PpWfVMHm0n-
WQRE2oos0tP-Kg20auBU

76. Covid-19 — Navigating the Uncharted: https://www.nejm.org/doi/
full/10.1056/nejme2002387?fbclid=IwAR3sRxm00vAjozZZKR7BBMFBX
u_5PfUQC1TzDudUPzuhEE0gi_2lsHb7qK8

77. N.C. 'Reporting Error' Fuels 200,000 COVID Testing Overcount: http://usnews.com/news/best-states/north-carolina/
articles/2020-08-12/nc-reporting-error-fuels-200-000-covid-testing-
overcount?src=usn_fb&fbclid=IwAR3C3byIMim3UTkXXKKxJ0Gm
pjS_T4O6vSnTGefzTQwO5ljEjQhiF2c6EOA

78. Japan Ends Coronavirus Emergency With 850 Deaths and No Lockdown:
https://www.newsweek.com/japan-ends-coronavirus-emergency-
850-deaths-no-lockdown-1506336?fbclid=IwAR2AAxkzMv0FNMMpPU8
c3sgQwwbrNjhrNg2hLYtQ1EVdZqJzGJOF60paQSw

79. Test for Past Infection (Antibody Test): https://www.newsweek.com/
japan-ends-coronavirus-emergency-850-deaths-no-lockdown-150633
6?fbclid=IwAR2AAxkzMv0FNMMpPU8c3sgQwwbrNjhrNg2hLYtQ1EVdZ
qJzGJOF60paQSw

80. CDC Tells States To Add Probable Coronavirus Cases: http://washingtontimes.com/news/2020/apr/15/cdc-tells-states-add-probable-coronavirus-cases

81. How CNN deceives readers: https://www.jeremyrhammond.com/2020/06/26/how-cnn-deceives-about-asymptomatic-transmission-of-sars-cov-2/

82. COVID-19 death rate is 75% lower in states that didn't lock down: WSJ: https://www.wnd.com/2020/06/covid-19-death-rate-75-lower-states-not-lock/

83. "The Blueprint For Liberty: Why And How We Could Restructure The United States In a Way That Pleases Everyone And Preserves Freedom - Kindle edition by Axelman, Elliot "Alu". Politics & Social Sciences Kindle eBooks @ Amazon.com: https://www.amazon.com/dp/B08X333FJ7/ref=sr_1_2?dchild=1&keywords=blueprint+for+liberty&qid=1613913432&s=digital-text&sr=1-2

ENDNOTES

1 https://www.gopusa.com/
   bofa-accused-of-helping-the-feds-ferret-out-conservatives
2 https://www.cnet.com/features/
   the-twisted-messy-hunt-for-covid-19s-origin-and-the-lab-leak-theory/
3 https://nypost.com/2020/08/11/
   facebook-removes-7-million-posts-for-false-covid-19-information/
4 https://fee.org/articles/
   the-origins-of-the-thought-police-and-why-they-scare-us/
5 https://www.businessinsider.com/the-us-government-and-
   the-sinaloa-cartel-2014-1?fbclid=IwAR3o31aAcBleFuqhBfhKHi
   5dX_Lesgtby1YqKuqmL2zLbX0YegOxQYsqBAo
6 https://libertyblock.com/a-manchin-of-corruption
7 https://www.redstate.com/stu-in-sd/2020/03/17/
   yes-mom-the-cdc-is-part-of-the-deep-state-too
8 https://www.webmd.com/cold-and-flu/cold-guide/common_cold_causes
9 https://www.cdc.gov/flu/about/burden/preliminary-in-season-estimates.
   htm
10 https://www.foxnews.com/media/
   physician-blasts-cdc-coronavirus-death-count-guidelines
11 https://www.facebook.com/texasnatmov/videos/958175417967369/
   UzpfSTU3MjY4NjA5MzoxMDE1NzYwMTYxNzgxNjA5NA/
12 https://coronavirus.jhu.edu/map.html
13 https://www.theblaze.com/op-ed/horowitz-more-evidence-coronavirus-flu
14 https://noqreport.com/2020/10/19/flu-cases-drop-95-compared-to-last-

year-are-patients-being-misdiagnosed-as-having-covid-19

15 https://www.lewrockwell.com/2020/12/joseph-mercola/
why-has-the-flu-disappeared

16 https://web.archive.org/web/20201126163323/https://www.jhunewsletter.
com/article/2020/11/a-closer-look-at-u-s-deaths-due-to-covid-19

17 https://politicofire.com/2020/11/30/horowitz-hopkins-analysis-showing-
covid-19-has-relatively-no-effect-on-deaths-in-us-retracted-from-publica-
tion-why

18 http://rt.com/news/488070-australia-us-coronavirus-suicide-spike/

19 https://www.foxnews.com/transcript/victor-davis-hanson-science-says-
children-rarely-get-coronavirus-they-arent-superspreaders

20 https://time.com/5816239/children-coronavirus/

21 https://www.theblaze.com/op-ed/ready-horowitz-norwegian-study-shows-
very-little-transmission-in-school-without-masks-as-suicide-crisis-intensifies

22 https://www.news.com.au/world/coronavirus/health/coronavirus-nsw-
study-shows-children-arent-spreading-covid19-to-other-kids/news-story/15
ce81cd9ee486e09143cd7fb426ef7b

23 https://www.reuters.com/article/
us-health-coronavirus-sweden-schools-idUSKCN24G2IS

24 https://www.cdc.gov/injury/wisqars/pdf/leading_causes_of_death_by_age_
group_2017-508.pdf

25 https://www.advisory.com/daily-briefing/2018/12/21/child-death

26 https://www.nbcnews.com/health/health-news/
more-1-million-children-u-s-have-had-covid-19-n1247913

27 https://downloads.aap.org/AAP/PDF/AAP%20and%20CHA%20-%20
Children%20and%20COVID-19%20State%20Data%20Report%202.11.21%20
FINAL.pdf

28 https://www.cdc.gov/flu/spotlights/2019-2020/2019-20-pediatric-flu-deaths.
htm

29 https://www.theblaze.com/op-ed/horowitz-large-wisconsin-study-shows-
almost-zero-virus-transmission-from-youth-sports

30 https://www.theblaze.com/op-ed/horowitz-more-evidence-coronavirus-flu

31 https://www.bbc.com/news/health-54616688

32 https://muchadoaboutcorona.ca/

lockdowns-causing-a-38-increase-in-opioid-deaths-and-sales/

33 https://www.rt.com/news/488070-australia-us-coronavirus-suicide-spike/

34 https://townhall.com/tipsheet/bronsonstocking/2020/11/28/one-country-saw-more-suicides-in-one-month-than-covid-deaths-all-year-long-n2580768

35 https://www.webmd.com/lung/news/20200512/covid19-lockdown-increases-child-abuse-risk

36 https://fee.org/articles/domestic-violence-more-than-doubled-under-lockdowns-new-study-finds/

37 https://www.nejm.org/doi/pdf/10.1056/NEJMsr180475

38 https://www.cdc.gov/injury/wisqars/pdf/leading_causes_of_death_by_age_group_2017-508.pdf

39 https://health.usnews.com/wellness/articles/hygiene-hypothesis-could-more-dirt-and-germs-boost-your-health

40 https://www.webmd.com/parenting/features/kids-and-dirt-germs#1

41 https://www.independent.co.uk/life-style/health-and-families/health-news/why-its-important-expose-kids-germs-scientist-explains-jack-gilbert-children-babies-immune-systems-a7845031.html

42 https://microbiome.uchicago.edu/

43 https://www.breitbart.com/europe/2021/02/27/german-psychiatrists-raise-alarm-on-lockdown-impact-on-childrens-mental-health/

44 https://youth-time.eu/to-talk-or-not-to-talk-that-is-the-question-at-least-70-percent-of-communication-is-non-verbal/

45 https://www.fox13memphis.com/news/local/should-you-wear-mask-home/NRQI5VQ2AVG7PFYN6FEQAHGC2Q/

46 https://www.cdc.gov/coronavirus/2019-ncov/daily-life-coping/using-trans-portation.html

47 https://www.nbcnews.com/shopping/wellness/cdc-masks-during-exercise-n1260261

48 https://www.msn.com/en-us/news/us/california-says-diners-should-wear-masks-between-bites/ar-BB19LEG4

49 https://amgreatness.com/2021/03/09/whistleblower-bidens-faa-forcing-air-traffic-controllers-to-wear-masks-while-speaking-to-pilots-causing-serious-read-back-errors

50 https://twitter.com/PhilHollowayEsq/status/1368703745488527362?ref_

src=twsrc%5Etfw%7Ctwcamp%5Etweetembed%7Ctwterm%5
E1368707267705573380%7Ctwgr%5E%7Ctwcon%5Es3_&ref_
url=https%3A%2F%2Famgreatness.com%2F2021%2F03%2F09%2Fwhis
tleblower-bidens-faa-forcing-air-traffic-controllers-to-wear-masks-while-
speaking-to-pilots-causing-serious-read-back-errors%2F

51 https://www.independent.co.uk/life-style/smiling-happy-expressions-mood-
mental-health-wellness-study-university-tennessee-a8866546.html

52 https://www.nbcnews.com/better/
health/6-immune-boosters-stave-colds-flu-ncna831201

53 https://townhall.com/tipsheet/micaelaburrow/2020/07/28/
redfield-says-more-abovebase-suicides-than-covid-deaths-n2573278

54 https://www.msn.com/en-us/news/watch/dermatolo-
gist-explains-why-face-masks-cause-acne-breakouts/
vp-BB173MYk

55 https://fee.org/articles/
new-danish-study-finds-masks-don-t-protect-wearers-from-covid-infection/

56 https://www.ncbi.nlm.nih.gov/pubmed/19216002

57 https://www.cambridge.org/core/journals/epidemiology-and-infection/arti-
cle/face-masks-to-prevent-transmission-of-influenza-virus-a-systematic-%20
review/64D368496EBDE0AFCC6639CCC9D8BC05

58 https://onlinelibrary.wiley.com/doi/epdf/10.1111/j.1750-2659.2011.00307.x

59 https://www.cmaj.ca/content/188/8/567

60 https://academic.oup.com/cid/article/65/11/1934/4068747

61 https://jamanetwork.com/journals/jama/fullarticle/2749214

62 https://onlinelibrary.wiley.com/doi/epdf/10.1111/jebm.12381

63 https://www.conservativereview.com/horowitz-comprehensive-analysis-of-
50-states-shows-greater-spread-with-mask-mandates-2649589520.html

64 https://news.northwestern.edu/stories/2021/01/
why-covid-19-pneumonia-worse-than-typical-pneumonia/

65 https://pubmed.ncbi.nlm.nih.gov/18500410/

66 https://en.wikipedia.org/wiki/Polycythemia

67 https://pubmed.ncbi.nlm.nih.gov/30848334/

68 https://www.huffpost.com/entry/the-disturbing-reality-of-
human-trafficking-and-children_b_58b1d696e4b0658fc20f9
5fa

69 https://libertyblock.com/cops-deserve-due-process-you-lowly-citizens-dont/

70 https://libertyblock.com/sununu-hints-at-banning-soda-mandating-exercise/

71 https://libertyblock.com/how-the-government-inflates-covid-statistics/

72 https://libertyblock.com/the-federal-reserve-is-killing-your-savings/

73 https://www.irishcentral.com/news/
robert-f-kennedy-jr-dr-fauci-covid19-vaccine

74 https://www.bizpacreview.com/2021/01/25/hundreds-of-scientists-
opposed-frankenstein-research-funded-by-fauci-that-may-link-to-
covid-19-1021027/

75 https://www.newsweek.com/dr-fauci-backed-controversial-wuhan-lab-
millions-us-dollars-risky-coronavirus-research-1500741

76 https://libertyblock.com/
breaking-governor-sununu-begins-to-mandate-masks/

77 https://libertyblock.com/
governor-sununu-mandates-contact-tracing-at-restaurants/

78 https://libertyblock.com/
sununu-wants-covid-agents-to-enter-property-without-warrants/

79 https://www.theblaze.com/op-ed/horowitz-ny-judge-releases-juvenile-
murder-suspect-a-second-time--after-he-allegedly-stabbed-a-woman

80 https://www.youtube.com/watch?v=1ehO57mMXjw

81 https://libertyblock.com/the-death-of-the-legislature/

82 https://canadafreepress.com/article/
the-cdc-confesses-to-lying-about-covid-19-death-numbers

83 https://www.dailywire.com/news/yes-hospitals-get-paid-more-for-coronavi-
rus-coded-patients-even-if-they-havent-been-tested

84 https://thespectator.info/2020/04/09/hospitals-get-paid-more-to-list-
patients-as-covid-19-and-three-times-as-much-if-the-patient-goes-on-
ventilator-video/

85 https://www.rollcall.com/2020/07/08/14m-in-relief-funds-
find-members-and-family/?fbclid=IwAR3kchbHtY0S6
7le4_e6zUQbUSHPCL4gLHh0BWfUHTeYaY-nXthsVNE5xTw

86 https://www.msn.com/en-us/news/politics/pence-chief-of-
staff-owns-stock-affected-by-bosss-coronavirus-work-report/
ar-BB14IEeY

87 https://libertyblock.com/covid-bill-redistributes-money-from-you-to-foreigners/

88 https://www.refinery29.com/en-us/2020/07/9904175/famous-ppp-loan-recipients-sba-list

89 https://www.nationalreview.com/news/senators-dumped-millions-in-stock-after-closed-door-briefing-on-coronavirus-records-show/

90 https://www.businessinsider.com/labour-johnson-government-must-stop-giving-coronavirus-contracts-tory-friends-2020-11

91 https://www.theguardian.com/politics/2020/nov/17/rishi-sunak-refuses-to-say-if-he-will-profit-from-moderna-covid-vaccine

92 https://www.opensecrets.org/orgs/wal-mart-stores/summary?id=D000000367

93 https://www.opensecrets.org/orgs/amazon-com/summary?id=D000023883

94 https://thefederalist.com/2020/06/25/until-zoom-breaks-with-communist-china-dont-use-it/

95 https://maritime-executive.com/article/wto-china-is-top-exporter-of-face-masks

96 https://townhall.com/tipsheet/bethbaumann/2021/03/21/watch-chris-wallace-and-dhs-secretary-mayorkas-spar-over-media-blackout-at-the-border-n2586600

97 https://pjmedia.com/news-and-politics/tyler-o-neil/2021/03/22/project-veritas-exposes-shocking-images-of-kids-packed-like-sardines-in-border-facility-n1434070

98 https://www.congress.gov/bill/116th-congress/house-bill/6553/text

99 https://www.foxnews.com/politics/rashida-tlaib-coronavirus-relief-checks-squad-abc-act

100 https://www.thebalance.com/fundamentals-of-the-2020-market-crash-4799950

101 https://www.fool.com/investing/2020/09/10/5-ways-the-stock-market-has-made-history-in-2020/

102 https://www.cbsnews.com/news/recession-linked-to-more-than-10000-suicides-in-north-america-europe/

103 https://www.washingtonpost.com/graphics/2020/business/coronavirus-recession-equality/

104 https://www.thebalance.com/
current-u-s-federal-government-tax-revenue-3305762

105 https://www.foxbusiness.com/economy/
us-spending-on-covid-relief-poised-to-hit-6t

106 https://libertyblock.com/the-us-is-already-a-democratic-socialist-nation/

107 https://www.cbsnews.com/news/how-capitalism-failed-us/

108 https://monthlyreview.org/2019/02/01/capitalism-has-failed-what-next/

109 https://monthlyreview.org/2019/02/01/capitalism-has-failed-what-next/

110 https://monthlyreview.org/2019/02/01/capitalism-has-failed-what-next/

111 https://electproject.github.io/Early-Vote-2020G/index.html

112 https://libertyblock.com/
legislation-makes-it-a-crime-to-disobey-citizen-mask-nazis/

113 https://disrn.com/news/wisconsin-dnr-tells-employees-to-wear-masks-
during-zoom-calls-at-home?fbclid=IwAR3Uxyl0b9olM5i2Wx9i8qReNXXXGs
MCo6kjzgP27tZ_ISAL_ZjmBkfrkt4

114 https://joemduncan.medium.com/
why-i-dont-feel-bad-when-anti-maskers-die-71d871f4bdda

115 https://trendingpolitics.com/i-want-to-beat-them-to-death-left-wing-
journalist-threatens-anti-maskers-christians-during-unhinged-rant/

116 https://en.wikipedia.org/wiki/List_of_people_burned_as_heretics

117 http://unamsanctamcatholicam.com/history/historical-apologetics/79-
history/596-scientists-executed-by-the-catholic-church.html

118 https://www.nbcnews.com/news/us-news/
california-pastor-church-found-contempt-fined-over-covid-rules-n1250481

119 https://www.bizpacreview.com/2020/10/12/orthodox-jewish-synagogues-
in-nyc-fined-15000-for-having-more-than-10-people-inside-983560/

120 https://nypost.com/2020/04/19/
three-arrested-outside-nyc-synagogue-after-violating-social-distancing/

121 https://www.buzzfeednews.com/article/dominicholden/
coronavirus-drive-in-church-mississippi-lawsuit-trump

122 https://trumpwhitehouse.archives.gov/articles/15-days-slow-spread/

123 https://www.newsmax.com/us/surgeon-general-adams-masks/2020/03/31/
id/960679/

124 https://www.thegatewaypundit.com/2020/10/cdc-first-said-not-wear-masks-wear-masks-masks-better-vaccines-now-new-evidence-shows-masks-dont-work/

125 https://saraacarter.com/jan-flashback-dr-fauci-said-coronavirus-is-not-a-major-threat-to-the-people-of-the-united-states/

126 https://youtu.be/ThSApOeeWiM

127 https://www.marketwatch.com/story/the-cdc-says-americans-dont-have-to-wear-facemasks-because-of-coronavirus-2020-01-30

128 https://www.forbes.com/sites/tarahaelle/2020/02/29/no-you-do-not-need-face-masks-for-coronavirus-they-might-increase-your-infection-risk/#57696323676c

129 http://dailymail.co.uk/news/article-8697125/Shocking-moment-bully-police-officer-PEPPER-SPRAYS-rail-passenger-resisting-arrest.html

130 https://youtu.be/8Pu-qjfbkyU

131 https://www.foxnews.com/health/coronavirus-idaho-womans-arrest-closed-playground-sparks-hundreds-protest

132 https://www.copblock.org/173784/update-parents-arrested-several-months-after-bringing-kids-to-concord-playground/

133 https://www.msn.com/en-us/health/medical/covid-19-deaths-reach-400-in-new-hampshire-data/ar-BB171BYm?fullscreen=true#image=1

134 https://www.israelnationalnews.com/News/News.aspx/286920

135 https://www.israelnationalnews.com/News/News.aspx/286920

136 https://www.nature.com/articles/s41467-020-19802-w

137 https://www.today.com/video/dr-fauci-double-masking-against-mutant-coronavirus-just-makes-common-sense-99959365958

138 https://www.urbandictionary.com/define.php?term=doubleplusgood

139 https://www.sacbee.com/news/coronavirus/article249697533.html

140 https://www.today.com/health/should-you-upgrade-your-face-mask-here-s-what-experts-t202567

141 https://nypost.com/2020/07/30/fauci-urges-americans-to-wear-goggles-for-added-covid-19-protection/

142 https://libertyblock.com/covid-vaccine-shows-promise-dems-upset-that-it-may-work/

143 https://www.doh.wa.gov/Newsroom/Articles/ID/2529/Over-1000-COVID-19-vaccine-doses-given-to-high-risk-health-workers-in-Washington-state-as-federal-changes-reduce-statewide-allocation

144 https://www.pfizer.com/news/press-release/press-release-detail/pfizer-and-biontech-conclude-phase-3-study-covid-19-vaccine

145 https://www.businessinsider.com/fauci-up-to-90-population-needs-vaccine-for-herd-immunity-2020-12

146 https://thepostmillennial.com/breaking-biden-says-if-americans-do-as-theyre-told-they-might-be-able-to-gather-for-the-4th-of-july

147 https://www.usatoday.com/in-depth/graphics/2021/01/14/covid-vaccine-distribution-by-state-how-many-covid-vaccines-have-been-given-in-us-how-many-people/6599531002/

148 https://www.washingtonexaminer.com/news/vaccine-means-masks-off-eventually

149 https://www.cnbc.com/2020/05/14/coronavirus-who-warns-it-could-take-up-to-5-years-to-control-pandemic.html

150 https://www.cnn.com/2021/03/10/health/coronavirus-variant-uk-more-deadly-study/index.html

151 https://www.cnn.com/2021/01/22/uk/uk-variant-scientists-johnson-intl/index.html

152 https://news.abs-cbn.com/news/03/22/21/uk-south-african-variant-cases-present-in-all-metro-manila-cities-doh

153 https://news.yahoo.com/uruguay-confirms-presence-brazilian-covid-233011579.html

154 https://www.scmp.com/yp/discover/news/global/article/3120653/coronavirus-there-are-4000-variants-virus-causes-covid-19

155 https://libertyblock.com/was-covid-the-catalyst-for-the-social-credit-system/

156 https://rumble.com/ves2df-rand-paul-and-dr.-fauci-get-into-giant-fight-in-middle-of-hearing-over-mask.html

157 https://libertyblock.com/yes-you-will-be-micro-chipped/

158 https://nypost.com/2020/07/24/anthony-fauci-denies-hypocrisy-after-watching-game-without-mask/

159 https://www.the-sun.com/news/2007123/dr-deborah-birx-family-thanksgiving-trip-hypocrisy/

160 https://www.youtube.com/watch?v=eY0g9eqQAmc

161 https://www.heritage.org/data-visualizations/public-health/covid-hypocrisy-policymakers-breaking-their-own-rules

162 https://www.youtube.com/watch?v=KrgqHfN18Co

163 http://thedailytimes.com/opinion/syndication/covid-hypocrisy-at-the-white-house/article_6f5e7abf-3663-5aac-a6b0-216080e8d8dc.html

164 https://www.nbcnews.com/health/health-news/black-lives-matter-protests-haven-t-led-covid-19-spikes-n1232045

165 https://www.newsweek.com/democrats-hypocrisy-riots-reveals-political-nature-coronavirus-lockdowns-opinion-1510325

166 https://prowhiteparty.wordpress.com/2020/07/15/blm-protests-and-riots-timeline-coincides-with-spike-in-covid-19-cases/

167 https://www.clickondetroit.com/news/local/2020/06/04/gov-whitmer-mayor-duggan-join-unity-march-through-detroit-in-honor-of-george-floyd/

168 https://atr.org/map

169 https://libertyblock.com/one-nation-divided/

170 https://libertyblock.com/sununu-hints-at-banning-soda-mandating-exercise

171 https://reason.com/2020/11/02/kamala-harris-equality-equity-outcomes

Made in United States
North Haven, CT
11 October 2021